A Firestorm Unleashed

JANUARY 1942 – JUNE 1943

By

Eleanor H. Ayer

Academic Editor:

Dr. William L. Shulman

President, Association of Holocaust Organizations
Director, Holocaust Resource Center & Archives, New York

Series Advisor:

Dr. Michael Berenbaum

President & CEO of Survivors of the
Shoah Visual History Foundation, Los Angeles

Series Editor:

Lisa Clyde Nielsen

Advisory Board:

Dr. Minton Goldman, Associate Professor of Political Science,
Northeastern University, Boston

Kathryn Schindler, Teacher, Laguna Niguel Middle School, California;
multicultural and tolerance educator

Kathryn Greenberg, Educational and public-administration specialist,
Chicago Department of Public Health, Division of School Health

Rachel Kubersky, BA Library Education, MPH

Joachim Kalter, Holocaust survivor

A   B L A C K B I R C H   P R E S S   B O O K

W O O D B R I D G E ,   C O N N E C T I C U T

Acknowledgments

Many people have given generously of their time and knowledge during the development of this series. We would like to thank the following people in particular: Genya Markon, and the staff at the United States Holocaust Memorial Museum Photo Archives—Leslie Swift, Sharon Muller, Alex Rossino, and Teresa Pollin—for their talented guidance; and Dr. Michael Berenbaum, currently President and CEO of the Survivors of the Shoah Visual History Foundation and formerly Director of the Research Institute at the U.S. Holocaust Memorial Museum, for his valuable editorial input and support of our efforts.

Dr. William L. Shulman, President of the Association of Holocaust Organizations and the Holocaust Resource Center & Archives at Queensborough Community College, merits special mention. As the series academic editor—as well as the compiler of Books 7 and 8—Dr. Shulman's guidance, insight, and dedication went far beyond the call of duty. His deep and thorough knowledge of the subject gave us all the critical perspective we needed to make this series a reality.

Published by Blackbirch Press, Inc.
260 Amity Road
Woodbridge, CT 06525

web site: http://www.blackbirch.com
e-mail: staff@blackbirch.com

©1998 Blackbirch Press, Inc.
First Edition

Printed in the United States of America

10 9 8 7 6 5 4 3 2 1

Cover: Captured Jews are marched to a deportation site during the Warsaw ghetto uprising in April 1943 (National Archives, courtesy USHMM Photo Archives).

Library of Congress Cataloging-in-Publication Data

Ayer, Eleanor H.
    A firestorm unleashed, January 1942 to June 1943 / by Eleanor H. Ayer.
        p.   cm. — (Holocaust)
    Includes bibliographical references and index.
    Summary: Explores the unique aspects and events in the period of the Holocaust between January 1942 and June 1943, blending historical narrative and primary sources.
        ISBN 1-56711-204-8 (alk. paper)
        1. World War, 1939–1945—Atrocities—Juvenile literature. 2. Genocide—Germany—History—20th century—Juvenile literature. 3. National socialism—Germany—Juvenile literature. 4. Jews—Persecutions—Germany—Juvenile literature. 5. Holocaust, Jewish (1939–1945)—Juvenile literature. [1. World War, 1939–1945—Atrocities. 2. Genocide. 3. Holocaust, Jewish (1939–1945)] I. Title. II. Series: Holocaust (Woodbridge, Conn.)
D804.G4A876   1998
940.53'18—dc21   96-44430
                                                                                  CIP
                                                                                  AC

CONTENTS

Preface

At the United States Holocaust Memorial Museum in Washington, D.C., a poignant documentary explores antisemitism and its role in the Holocaust. The film ends with these words:

THIS IS WHERE PREJUDICE CAN LEAD.

That somber warning has guided our work on this series.

The task of creating a series of books on the Holocaust seemed, at first, straightforward enough: We would develop an in-depth account of one of the most complex and compelling periods in human history.

But it quickly became clear to us that, on an emotional level, this series would not be straightforward at all. Indeed, the more work we did, the more we realized just how this subject wraps itself around everyone it touches. As we discussed content with our authors and advisors and began to select photographs and other documents for reproduction, several unanticipated and complicated issues arose.

The first major issue was pivotal, in that our decision would guide the content of the books: How should we choose to define the very term *Holocaust?* Many scholars of the Holocaust believe that the term should be used exclusively in reference to the approximately 6 million European Jews who were murdered by Nazis and their collaborators between 1933 and 1945. This is because no other group was singled out so systematically and relentlessly for genocide. Should the perhaps 4 million non-Jewish victims of the period—the Soviet prisoners of war, Romani (Gypsies), Jehovah's Witnesses, German and Austrian male homosexuals, and other groups—be discussed on the same level as the Jews? Ultimately—in philosophical agreement with the U.S. Holocaust Memorial Museum—we decided to focus our discussion primarily on the Jews but also to report the experiences of other victims.

Our second major decision had to do with how to present the material. How explicit should the books be in their written descriptions and photographic records of what was done to the victims? Perhaps never before have the brutalities of war and the consequences of prejudice and hatred been so extensively chronicled; perhaps never so eloquently and, at the same time, in such painful detail.

On this issue, we decided we would chronicle what happened, but try not to shock or horrify. Learning about the Holocaust should be disturbing—but there is a delicate line between informative realism and sensationalism. The most brutal accounts and documentation of the Holocaust can be found in many other sources; we believe that in our series, much of this story will be revealed through the powerful and moving images we have selected.

Yet another difficult issue was raised by our educational advisors: Was the Holocaust truly a singular historical event, uniquely qualified for such detailed study as is provided in this series? That it was an extraordinary period in history, there can be no denial—despite some misguided people's efforts to the contrary. Certainly, never before had an entire nation organized its power and mobilized itself so efficiently for the sole purpose of destroying human life. Yet the Holocaust was not unique in terms of the number of people murdered; nor was it unique in the brutality of the hatred on which it fed.

A subject such as this raises many questions. How could the Holocaust have happened? Could it have been prevented? How can we keep this from happening again? We have done our best to explore the questions we feel are most central. Ultimately, however, the most compelling questions to emerge from learning about the Holocaust are for each individual reader to answer.

Foreword

There is a paradox in the study of the Holocaust: The more distant we are from the Event, the more interest seems to grow. In the immediate aftermath of the Holocaust, horrific images were played in movie theaters on newsreels, which was how people saw the news in an era before television. Broadcasting on CBS radio, famed newscaster Edward R. Murrow said:

> *Permit me to tell you what you would have seen and heard had you been with me on Thursday. It will not be pleasant listening. If you are at lunch or have no appetite to hear of what Germans have done, now is a good time to turn off your radio, for I propose to tell you of Buchenwald.*

Murrow described the sights and sounds of what he had experienced in the immediate aftermath of liberation, and his audience was appropriately horrified. Action was required, trials were soon held—an accounting for a deed that was beyond human comprehension, a crime beyond a name, that we now call the "Holocaust."

Shortly thereafter, interest waned. Other topics of the era took center stage—the Cold War, the Berlin blockade, the Korean War—and it seemed for a time that the Holocaust would be forgotten. In retrospect, we can surmise that the silence was a necessary response to such catastrophe. Distance was needed before we could look back and muster enough courage to confront an event so terrible.

No one could have imagined that, half a century after the Holocaust, museums such as the United States Holocaust Memorial Museum would be built and would attract millions of visitors each year. No one, too, would have guessed that films such as *Schindler's List* would be seen by tens of millions of people throughout the world. No one could have foreseen that thousands of books would be published on the subject and courses in schools all over the world would be taught—that interest in this horrible chapter of history would intensify rather than recede with the passage of time.

Why study the Holocaust?

The answer is simple: Because it happened!

An event of such magnitude, a state-sponsored annihilation of an entire people—men, women, and children—must be confronted. Some people have portrayed the Holocaust as an aberration, a world apart from the ordinary world in which we dwell. Even the most eloquent of survivors, Elie Wiesel, calls it the "Kingdom of Night." Yet, to me the Holocaust is not an aberration, but an expression in the extreme of a common thread that runs through our civilization. And thus, not to confront the Event is not to probe the deep darkness that is possible within our world.

Because it happened, we must seek to understand the anguish of the victims—the men, women, and children who faced death and had impossible choices to make, and who could do so little to determine their fate. And we must seek to understand the neutrality and indifference of the bystanders around the world; and what caused the Allies—who were fighting a full-scale world war against the Germans and other Axis powers—to fail to address the "second war," the war against the Jews.

We must also seek to understand the all-too-few non-Jewish heroes of the Holocaust—the men, women, and children who opened their homes and their hearts and provided a haven for the victims; a place to sleep, a crust of bread, a kind word, a hiding place. What makes such goodness possible? Why were they immune to the infection of evil?

We must understand that the Holocaust did not begin with mass killing. Age-old prejudice led to discrimination, discrimination led to persecution, persecution to incarceration, incarceration to annihilation. And mass murder, which culminated with the killing of approximately 6 million Jews, did not begin with the Jews—nor did it encompass only the Jews. The state-sponsored murder of the physically and mentally disabled was a precursor to the Holocaust. It was in that killing process that gas chambers and crematoria were developed and refined, and the staff of the death camps were trained. Romani (commonly but incorrectly referred to as Gypsies) were killed alongside the Jews. Jehovah's Witnesses, German and Austrian male homosexuals, political prisoners and dissidents were also incarcerated in concentration camps, where many were murdered. Gentile and Jewish Poles were subjected to decimation and destruction of their national identity. Though many Jews suffered alone, abandoned and forgotten by the world, they were not the only ones to die.

The study of the Holocaust is not easy. We are often unclear about whose history is being taught: German history, Jewish history, American history, European history. And to understand it, we need to understand more than history. Other disciplines are essential, such as psychology and sociology, political science, philosophy and theology, and most especially, ethics. When we study the Holocaust, we are forced to face evil, to confront experiences that are horrific and destructive. And even despite the tools of all these disciplines, we still may not understand. Comprehension may elude us.

With the renewed interest in the Holocaust—especially in North America—we have seen that the study of all these deaths is actually in the service of life; the study of evil actually strengthens decency and goodness. For us as free citizens, confronting this European event brings us a new recognition of the principles of constitutional democracy: A belief in equality and equal justice under law; a commitment to pluralism and toleration; a determination to restrain government by checks and balances and by the constitutional protection of "inalienable rights;" and a struggle for human rights as a core value.

The Holocaust shatters the myth of innocence, and, at the same time, has implications for the exercise of power. Those who wrestle with its darkness know it can happen again—even in the most advanced, most cultured, most "civilized" of societies. But, if we are faithful to the best of human values, the most sterling of our traditions, then we can have confidence that it "won't happen here." These truths are not self-evident; they are precarious and, therefore, even more precious.

The Holocaust has implications for us as individuals. As we read these books, we can't help but ask ourselves, "What would I have done?" "If I were a Jew, would I have had the courage to resist—spiritually or militarily—and when?" "Would I have had the wisdom and the ability to flee to a place that offered a haven?" "Do I have a friend who would offer me a place of shelter, a piece of bread, a moment of refuge?" "What could I have done to protect my family, to preserve my life?"

We can't offer easy answers because the options were few, the pressures extreme, the conditions unbearable, and the stakes ultimate—life or death.

We may also ask ourselves even more difficult questions: "What prejudices do I have?" "Do I treat all people with full human dignity?" "Am I willing to discriminate against some, to scapegoat others?" "Am I certain—truly certain—that I could not be a killer? That I would not submit to the pressures of conformity and participate in horrible deeds or, worse yet, embrace a belief that makes me certain—absolutely certain—that I am right and the others are wrong? That my cause is just and the other is an enemy who threatens me, who must be eliminated?" These are questions you will ask as you read these books—ask, but not answer.

Perhaps, in truth, the more intensely you read these books, the less certainty you will have in offering your personal answer. Premature answers are often immature answers. Good questions invite one to struggle with basic values.

The central theme of the story of the Holocaust is not regeneration and rebirth, goodness or resistance, liberation or justice, but, rather, death and destruction, dehumanization and devastation, and above all, loss.

The killers were "civilized" men and women of an advanced culture. They were both ordinary and extraordinary, a true cross-section of the men and women of Germany, its allies, and their collaborators, as well as the best and the brightest. In these volumes, those deeds will be seen, as will the evolution of policy, the expansion of the power of the state, and technological and scientific murders unchecked by moral, social, religious, or political constraints. Whether restricted to the past or a harbinger of the future, the killers demonstrated that systematic mass destruction is possible. Under contemporary conditions, the execution of such a policy would only be easier.

The Holocaust transforms our understanding. It shatters faith—religious faith in God and secular faith in human goodness. Its truth has been told not to provide answers, but to raise questions. To live conscientiously in its aftermath, one must confront the reality of radical evil and its past triumphs. At the same time, we must fight against that evil and its potential triumphs in the future.

The call from the victims—from the world of the dead—is to remember. From the survivors, initial silence has given way to testimony. The burden of memory has been transmitted and thus shared. From scholars, philosophers, poets, and artists—those who were there and those who were not—we hear the urgency of memory, its agony and anguish, its meaning and the absence of meaning. To live in our age, one must face the void.

Israel Ba'al Shem Tov, the founder of Hasidism, once said:

In forgetfulness is the root of exile.
In remembrance, the seed of
redemption.

His fears of forgetting, we understand all too well.

Whether we can share his hope of remembrance is uncertain.

Still, it is up to us to create that hope.

Michael Berenbaum
Survivors of the Shoah
Visual History Foundation
Los Angeles, California

"Only Carrying Out Orders"

New Year's Day of 1942 was one of promise and optimism throughout the Third Reich, the vast German empire created by Adolf Hitler. The *Führer*, as Germany's leader was called, had predicted that his Reich would last at least a thousand years. At the beginning of 1942, it seemed that his prediction might come true. Germany, headed by Hitler and the National Socialist German Workers' Party—the Nazi Party—had already taken control of much of Europe.

Since World War II had begun, on September 1, 1939, German Army, Navy, and Air Force (*Luftwaffe*) troops had been successful in most of their major campaigns. Territory stretching from the Scandinavian countries all the way to North Africa, and from France eastward into the Soviet Union, had been conquered swiftly, and in many cases with little fighting.

A Russian Jew kneels at the edge of a mass grave seconds before he is shot by a German member of the *Einsatzgruppen*. It is estimated that one-quarter of all Jews who perished in the Holocaust were murdered by mobile killing squads in this way.

In December 1941, the United States had entered the war on the side of the Allies, joining Great Britain, France, and the Soviet Union in their fight against the Axis powers—led by Germany, Italy, and Japan. Even at that time, despite the fact that Hitler was fighting a world war, he still remained absorbed in determining the fate of the Jewish people, whom he called "cold-hearted, shameless, and calculating."

The Jews of Europe, claimed Hitler, were responsible for Germany's defeat in World War I and for all the problems that had befallen the country since then: inflation, unemployment, poverty, and hunger.

For years, Hitler had made his antisemitism—hatred of Jews— well known. But so radical were his ideas that few people could take him seriously. "The Jew must clear out of Europe," he told Heinrich Himmler, head of the SS (for *Schutzstaffel*; SS men were often called "black-shirts"). The SS was the Nazi "protection squad," the single most powerful organization in the Third Reich. "If they refuse to go voluntarily," said Hitler, "I see no other solution but extermination." Helping Hitler to achieve this goal, which would be termed the "Final Solution," would be the Gestapo, the secret-police arm of the SS. The Gestapo later rounded up and arrested the Jews of Europe, who would be "deported"—sent either to death (extermination) or labor (concentration) camps.

Many ordinary German people also aided the Nazis in their plan to make Europe *Judenrein,* a Nazi term meaning "purified of Jews." Some did nothing more than ignore the mistreatment of their Jewish neighbors. But standing idly by, even without taking an active part in the persecution of the Jews, encouraged the Nazis to pursue their goal of exterminating them. Other citizens willingly joined the Nazi Party and soon found themselves in positions of power and prestige. Many became guards in the camps, members of the SS or Gestapo, or informers against the Jews.

The man whom Hitler put in charge of arranging transportation for the millions of deportees was Adolf Eichmann. An SS lieutenant colonel, Eichmann headed the Department of Jewish Affairs. As such, he played a key role in the murder of European Jews, most especially those who were killed in the camps. But at his later trial, he excused himself from blame by arguing that he was "only carrying out orders." The "Popes of the Third Reich" have spoken, Eichmann would say, referring to his Nazi superiors. "Who am I to have my own thoughts?"

In January 1942, Eichmann met with 14 other SS officials to develop a detailed blueprint for genocide, a plan for murdering all the Jews of Europe—exterminating them by literally the hundreds of thousands. The meet-

Reinhard Heydrich was responsible for implementing Hitler's genocide plan that eventually became known as the Nazis' "Final Solution."

ing was led by high-ranking Nazi official Reinhard Heydrich. Heydrich's ideas for implementing genocide, as handed down from Hitler, became what the Nazis called the "Final Solution of the Jewish Question."

Over the next three and a half years, the Jews of Europe were shipped to their deaths in unbelievable numbers. Some were killed by the Gestapo in the streets of the ghettos—special sections of cities where Jews were forced to live in cramped, filthy conditions. Others were taken from their homes and worked to death in concentration camps. Many Jews were sent immediately to gas chambers at the newly established death camps in German-occupied Poland.

In addition to the approximately 6 million Jews who were killed, countless millions of other lives would be forever affected by the Holocaust. Children born after the war to survivors grew up with a complex and often painful legacy of intense guilt and anger. These children were to be constant, living reminders of relatives they had never known—of family who had been murdered in the Holocaust, one of the darkest periods in all human history.

"Resettlement"

Above the Wall of Remembrance at the United States Holocaust Memorial Museum in Washington, D.C., large letters spell out this message:

THE FIRST TO PERISH WERE THE CHILDREN. . . . FROM THESE THE NEW DAWN MIGHT HAVE RISEN

The words are a grim reminder that, of the millions of Jews who were murdered by Adolf Hitler's Nazis, the children were among the first to die. Their youth and innocence did not spare them from Hitler's death camps. Of the children, only the older teenagers—those who might be useful to the Nazis as slaves— were kept alive.

A German Jew, carrying all his remaining belongings, waits at an assembly point for deportation to the Chelmno death camp in 1942.

The First Death Camp Opens

By December 1941, one of Hitler's concerns became the systematic killing of the Jews and other groups, many of whom the Nazis called *Untermenschen*—"subhumans," people whom they considered undesirable. These included the Romani (commonly but incorrectly called Gypsies), the physically and mentally

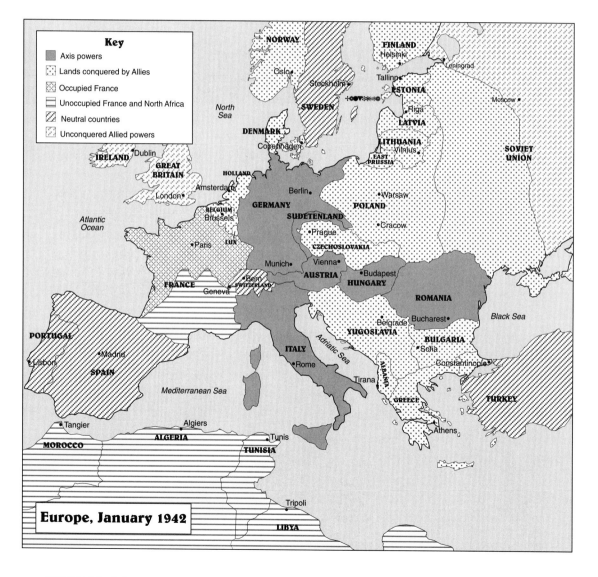

Key

- Axis powers
- Lands conquered by Allies
- Occupied France
- Unoccupied France and North Africa
- Neutral countries
- Unconquered Allied powers

Europe, January 1942

Above: Jews from the Lodz ghetto board the freight cars that will take them to the death camp at Chelmno in the spring of 1942.

Below: Open freight cars packed with people arrive at Chelmno, 1942.

disabled, German male homosexuals, political prisoners, and others who were judged "inferior" or "defective" by Hitler and his colleagues. Perhaps as many as 4 million of these people would be murdered by the Nazis and their collaborators.

On December 8, gassing of human beings began at Chelmno, the first of the six extermination camps in German-occupied Poland, amid great secrecy. Although the highest-ranking Nazis had been contemplating mass murder for some time, they wanted no one to know the details of their plans. At Chelmno, less than 35 miles (56 kilometers) from the German-occupied Polish city of Lodz, more than 300,000 people would be murdered, most of them Jews. Fewer than 10 people sent to Chelmno are known to have survived. At its peak, more than 1,000 Jews per day were murdered at this killing center.

To carry out this genocide required not only the direction of Nazi leaders but also the participation of thousands of workers to execute the direction of and dispose of the bodies. Members of the SS usually carried out the killings, most often by gassing or shooting the victims. Some Jewish prisoners in the camps were even forced to bury the bodies or load them into ovens for burning.

Shortly after the Chelmno death camp opened, Adolf Eichmann, charged with shipping victims to the camps, was called there by a Gestapo chief to watch the way in which guards disposed of the bodies. Even Eichmann was horrified by what he witnessed at Chelmno. "I couldn't speak," he confessed in a later report. "I had to get away. Frightful, I tell you. An inferno. Can't do it. I can't do it."

The *Einsatzgruppen*

With the help of the *Einsatzgruppen*, however, the Nazis did do it. The *Einsatzgruppen* were mobile killing squads—"Special Action Groups" organized by SS chief Heinrich Himmler and his associate, Reinhard Heydrich. The groups' main purpose was to kill enemies of the Reich, particularly Jews and Communists.

The *Einsatzgruppen* consisted of several thousand men divided into units of 800 to 1,200. They had orders to follow the victorious German Army into Poland and the Soviet Union and to exterminate all the Jews and Communists they could find.

Upon entering a town, members of the *Einsatzgruppen* would order a few prominent Jewish citizens to round up all Jews. This was referred to as an *Aktion*, an "action" against the Jews. The captives would be sent east to German-occupied lands "for resettlement," the Nazis stated matter-of-factly. Most Jews did as they were told—many suspected nothing serious—but soon they learned that the promise of being "resettled" in another location was a cruel lie. Instead, the Jews of the town were shot and their bodies were thrown into huge ditches. H.F. Graebe, a German

A crowd watches members of the *Einsatzgruppen* execute four Jews near Kovno, Lithuania, in 1942.

engineer who tried to save the lives of his Jewish employees, witnessed one of the *Einsatzgruppen* massacres:

> *The people . . . had to undress upon the order of an SS man, who carried a riding or dog whip. They had to put their clothes in separate piles of shoes, top clothing and underclothing. . . . Without screaming or weeping these people undressed, stood in family groups, kissed each other, said their farewells, and waited for a sign from another SS man, who stood near the pit [into which the victims fell], also with a whip in his hand. . . .*

So efficient were the *Einsatzgruppen's* mass murders that the Nazis soon had to devise new ways to dispose of the dead. There were so many bodies that, even after burial, they emanated a hideous smell and caused the spread of disease. To solve this problem, *Einsatzgruppen* commander Paul Blobel developed a body-disposal method at the Chelmno camp. There, he built a furnace that was fueled by chopped wood and corpses:

> *The furnace could hold 100 corpses at a time, but as they burnt down, fresh ones were added from above. . . . The ashes and remains of bones were removed from the ash-pit, and ground in mortars, and, at first, thrown into specially dug ditches; but later . . . [they were] thrown into the river.*

The Wannsee Conference

Adolf Hitler had nurtured his hatred of Jews for two decades. In a letter to a German Army agent soon after World War I ended in 1918, he outlined "the proper attitude to be cultivated toward the Jews." He accused Jews of being the cause of Germany's troubles during the war and suggested that "the final aim [of government] must be the deliberate removal of the Jews."

On January 20, 1942, a conference was held in Wannsee, a suburb of the German capital, Berlin. Headed by Reinhard Heydrich, the purpose of the meeting was to find a "solution to the Jewish question in Europe." Heydrich estimated that this "question" involved 11 million Jews. The SS and government officials who were present decided that it was "advisable to eliminate the Jews as rapidly as possible since they [posed] both health and economic hazards."

Adolf Eichmann is thought to have recorded the events of the meeting. During the meeting, participants talked freely about "extermination" and "liquidation," but apparently the words "murder" and "genocide" were never mentioned. Instead, they talked in code words, speaking of "resettlement" and the "Final Solution."

Nazi orders specified that, "For the moment, the evacuated Jews will be brought bit by bit to so-called transit ghettos from where they will be transported farther to the east." Eastern Europe was where the Nazis built not only their death camps but also many of their labor camps and factories. The resettled prisoners provided a large workforce. Organizers admitted, however, that "a large part [of resettled Jews] will fall away through natural reduction." In other words, officials expected that huge numbers of Jews would be killed by overwork, starvation, and disease.

Deportations Increase

Before the Wannsee Conference, one death camp and a few dozen concentration camps were already in operation. At Wannsee, Heydrich produced a list of the number of Jews in each European country. After that, deportations increased. The Jews of White Russia (today, Belarus, just east of Poland) and Crimea (a peninsula on the Black Sea) were targeted immediately. These areas had come under Nazi control after the German invasion of the Soviet Union in June 1941. From January through mid-April 1942, nearly 100,000 Crimean Jews were killed—enough to satisfy the SS that "the Crimea is purged of Jews."

The Nazis' ambitions to murder the Jews soon extended to the other parts of Europe that were under their control. Heydrich estimated Finland's Jewish population at 2,300. At first, the Finnish government went along with the Nazis' deportation orders. But when officials learned that the first 11 people were deported not

Himmler's Notion of "Humane Murder"

Himmler

While he was visiting a murder site in the summer of 1942, SS chief Heinrich Himmler was horrified by the slow, torturous way two Jewish women died during a mass shooting. Henceforth, Himmler ordered, women and children would not be shot but would be murdered more "humanely" in gas vans to be used by the *Einsat-26 zgruppen*. His concern, however, was not for the victims. He was worried about the effects on the *Einsatzgruppen* who carried out the killings.

These large, ordinary vans looked like closed trucks, but when the driver pressed the accelerator, carbon-monoxide gas was pumped into the back where

Mobile killing van.

Jewish men await death in a gas van.

the prisoners were loaded. It took 10 to 15 minutes for the 15 to 25 "passengers" in each van to die.

The vans, however, posed problems for the Nazis. According to a Dr. Becker, who was in charge of constructing them, "Persons to be executed suffer death from suffocation and not death by dozing off, as was planned." It was a "great ordeal," he said, for the *Einsatzgruppen* to bury people who had suffocated. It caused "immense psychological injuries and damage to their [the *Einsatzgruppen's*] health." Consequently, Dr. Becker readjusted the vans' levers to ensure that prisoners would fall asleep—to their deaths.

for labor but for death, they refused to send any more. Deportations from elsewhere in the Reich were staggering in number.

The targeted Jews in each country were told only that they were being "resettled." They were not told where they were going or for what purpose, because the Nazis did not want rumor and panic to spread. Initially, some Jews believed that a better or more stable life awaited them. Others didn't understand what was going on, but they saw no choice but to obey orders.

Resistance Grows

It is sometimes said that Jews of the Holocaust went passively to their deaths, like sheep to the slaughter, without putting up a fight. There are many factors that may have contributed to that appearance. Jews had been the victims of antisemitism for nearly 2,000 years before the Holocaust, and generally they had adapted by negotiation, not by fighting. For centuries, this had been a traditional Jewish way: to negotiate, to bargain with enemies, to find a workable solution, to adapt to adverse conditions.

But to say that the Jews went passively to their deaths is simply not true. Many people, particularly youths, resisted fiercely. As deportations increased, so did the number of resistance groups. Some members of the resistance were Jews, some were non-Jews. The goal of most groups was to resist the Germans and disrupt their operations as much as possible. They set fire to German military bases, stole weapons or uniforms; some even blew up restaurants or taverns known to be frequented by German officers. By so doing, they hoped to create a feeling of chaos and disorder, thereby bringing a quicker end to the war.

For one group, the Bielski Partisans, the primary goal was not only to disrupt German operations or kill Nazis, but to save Jewish lives. The Bielskis, who operated in the western portion of White Russia, were one of the largest and most successful partisan groups—groups of independent fighters against the Nazis. Their leader was Tuvia Bielski. He believed it was more important to save one Jew than to kill 20 Germans. He proved this by

A group portrait in the "family camp" of the Bielski Partisans.

taking into his group the sick, the young, and the elderly—people who would be of little use in fighting the Germans but who needed protection from them. When asked how he planned to get food for so many people who could not fight, Tuvia replied in a calm, assured manner:

> *Why do you worry so much about food. Let the peasants worry. We will get [steal] what we need from the peasants and let more Jews come. . . . Would that there were thousands of Jews who could reach our camp, we would take all of them in.*

Tuvia's own parents, wife, and two brothers were murdered by the Nazis. But out of his sorrow came determination that eventually grew into a "forest community"—a home in the woods for more than 1,200 resisters. It was the most massive rescue operation of Jews by Jews during the Holocaust.

Escape from Europe

Many other Jews tried desperately to flee Europe. But many countries, including the United States, had set quotas, or limits, on immigration. This meant that only a certain number of Jews from Europe could enter a country in a given year; and in most cases, this number was quite small. Many Jews, frustrated by the quota system and by the antisemitism elsewhere in the world, began looking at Palestine (part of which is now the State of Israel), which they considered their ancestral homeland. There, they believed, they could find permanent refuge from the persecution in Europe.

At that time, the British government controlled Palestine. The country was populated largely by Arabs who did not want the Jews overtaking what Arabs also considered to be their homeland. To keep peace with the Arabs, on whom Britain relied for much of its oil, the British government drew up the "White Paper" in 1939. This ruling put a quota on the number of Jews who could emigrate to Palestine. Many Jews, however, chose to ignore the rule and tried to enter the country illegally.

A popular escape route to Palestine was from Romania, across the Black Sea to Turkey, through the Dardanelles Strait, and across the Mediterranean Sea. Jewish refugees went to Romania hoping to get space on a ship bound for Palestine.

On December 12, 1941, the ship *Struma* left Romania on this route. But when it docked in Istanbul, Turkey, British officials put pressure on the Turkish government to make the ship turn back, to avoid trouble with the Arabs. Adrift in the Black Sea, the *Struma* was torpedoed and sunk, most likely by the Germans, on February 24, 1942. All but one of the 769 people aboard drowned, most of them Jews.

Throughout the war, and even after it ended, the British government continued to make it difficult for Jews to enter Palestine. It seemed that even the Jews who were fortunate enough to escape the terror of Eastern Europe were doomed no matter where they went.

"So Many People at Once"

As the pace of deportations from Germany increased, trains began running regularly from the ghettos and concentration camps to the death camps in German-occupied Poland. Helga Weissova-Hoskova was one of thousands of teenagers at Theresienstadt, a concentration camp in German-occupied Czechoslovakia. Although she suffered greatly there, she grieved more for the elderly people around her who were being sent to the death camps. Later, in *Terezin Diary*, she wrote:

> . . . *Old people's transport. Ten thousand sick, crippled, dying, all of them over 65 years old. . . . Why do they want to send these defenseless people away? If they want to get rid of us young people, I can understand that. . . . But how can these old people be dangerous? [Why] can't they let them die in peace here?*

Thousands of men stand in formation for roll call at the Buchenwald camp.

"A Ghetto for the Aged"

According to Nazi propaganda, Theresienstadt was a place where the elderly could die in peace. When it opened in November 1941, the high-ranking Nazi Reinhard Heydrich described the facilities as "a ghetto for the aged." One section was designed as a place where foreign officials and Red Cross workers could "see" how well the Germans treated their prisoners. "A spa for the aged and privileged Jews" was how the Germans promoted Theresienstadt. Prominent Jews and Jewish war heroes, as well as wealthy people who could pay, were supposedly "privileged" to live here. "Old German Jews brought with them their top hats, tails, lace dresses, and parasols," wrote historian Konnilyn Feig, for they expected this to be a sort of vacation resort.

In their effort to deceive the world into believing the Theresienstadt camp was an independent Jewish city, Nazis printed and issued this currency, which had no value.

But within a few months, the Nazi "showplace" had become a horribly overcrowded transit center. Like other such centers, it was no longer a final destination but a temporary way station for prisoners on their way to other camps. During 1942, as many as 90,000 Jews were sent to Theresienstadt to live in a space designed for 7,000 people. Food shortages caused starvation and disease—sanitary conditions were nonexistent. Dozens of people had to share one toilet. By September 1942, the rate of death was 131 people per day. Noted Feig: "Many times a day the residents watched the carts loaded with plank coffins passing through the streets on their way to the mass graves."

Conditions were equally severe in the ghettos of Eastern Europe—the sections of cities where Jews were forced to live. At the ghetto in Radom, Poland, on a day that became known as "Bloody Thursday," Nazis shot 40 people on the street. On March 2, 1942, in the Russian ghetto of Minsk, approximately 5,000 Jews were taken to the edge of town to a huge, freshly dug pit. There, soldiers machine-gunned the adults, who fell into a common grave. Children were thrown alive into the pit to die of suffocation.

Belzec Opens

As deportations increased in 1942, new extermination camps were opened. Beginning on March 17, an estimated 15,000 Jews were deported from the ghetto in Lublin—in German-occupied Poland—to a new camp at Belzec. The second of the death centers, Belzec had been opened that very day. In the first wave of killing there, more than 6,700 people died.

Belzec was not a concentration camp; it was solely meant for murder. There were no facilities for housing prisoners, because no one stayed overnight. Said a member of the Polish resistance movement, "The common report was that every Jew who reached it, without exception, was doomed to death." Belzec was the first of three killing centers along Poland's Bug River, and it quickly became fully operational. During its first week, nearly all the Jews of Lublin were deported there and gassed to death. In an *Aktion* that began on March 15 and lasted several days, approximately 15,000 Jews from Lvov, in eastern Poland, were sent to Belzec and killed.

Belzec was the first center to have permanent gas chambers. Together, its six sections could kill 15,000 people a day. The deadly gas it used was carbon monoxide. At that point, there were no crematoria—ovens in which to burn the bodies. The dead were simply thrown into mass graves.

At the Chelmno death camp, that practice soon posed a problem: The ground started heaving from the chemicals released naturally by the decaying bodies. This created an especially grotesque scene, and eventually the Nazis were forced to unearth the mass graves and burn the bodies.

Nearly all of Belzec's 600,000 victims were Jews, but 1,200 Gentile (non-Jewish) Poles were also murdered there. Of all those who were deported to Belzec, only two people are known to have survived. One of them, Chaim Hirschmann, was killed in an antisemitic incident in Lublin, Poland, less than a year after the end of World War II.

Resistance in Vain

As the killings increased, more and more people took steps to save themselves. For many of the Jews, death by resistance was far preferable to dying without a fight in a Nazi extermination camp. Most, however, were powerless against the Nazis. No Jew was allowed to have guns or other weapons. Most were isolated from the outside world, so planning any action became nearly impossible. Because of these severe limitations, many young, single Jews escaped to join partisan or other resistance groups, which they considered better than waiting for deportation. But partisans faced capture or attack by German forces that were much better armed and trained than they, making their chances of survival slim. A partisan's life was very dangerous and nerve-wracking. In addition to the obvious dangers, they faced the added disadvantages of being easily recognized and having no support from the citizens at large. Instead of finding safety in the outside world, they were more vulnerable there. Still, for many, the opportunity to take some control of the future outweighed the risks of capture.

Near Ilja, in a German-occupied part of the Soviet Union, a group of Jewish prisoners, sent by the Nazis to do farm work, decided to run away. When SS officials found that the prisoners were missing and learned that they had joined a partisan group, they were outraged. To teach the Jews in surrounding communities a lesson, the SS shot all of Ilja's sick and elderly Jews in the street. The remaining 900 residents were forced into a building, which the Nazis locked and set afire. Everyone inside burned to death.

Those who managed to join resistance groups or partisan units found that escaping from the ghettos or concentration camps was only the first of many hurdles. Once free, they faced the problem of finding food, which was in short supply. Usually, local towns-people were too afraid to befriend the escapees or share food with them, because the penalty for helping or harboring a Jew was death or deportation. And in many areas, antisemitism was so strong that escaped Jews found themselves in just as much danger from villagers as they were at the hands of the Nazis.

Joining a partisan band was only one way in which Jews resisted. In the ghettos and concentration camps, as transports to the death centers became more frequent, residents often banded together to stage an uprising, with the hope of escaping. In the German-occupied town of Lakhwa, Poland, home to approximately 2,300 Jews, a ghetto was established in April 1942. Immediately, young people began holding meetings to plan resistance. They collected tools and scraps that could be used as weapons: axes, hammers, pitchforks, and metal pipes. The Nazis surrounded the ghetto on September 3 and ordered all buildings burned to the ground. While the fires were raging, Jews attacked the Nazis with their crude weapons, and many of them were able to get out of the ghetto. Only about 120, however, managed to reach safety in the nearby forests—the townspeople had joined the Nazis in hunting down escapees and shooting them.

Auschwitz–Birkenau

With Hitler's Final Solution growing in intensity, and deportations reaching new highs, the SS found that it needed faster and more efficient methods of killing people. Near the German-occupied Polish town of Oświecim ("Auschwitz" in German), a labor camp housing mostly Polish political prisoners had been in operation since April 1940. It was called Auschwitz. In October 1941, a second camp, Auschwitz II–Birkenau, opened. Birkenau became a killing center. Seven months later, a third camp was opened: Auschwitz III–Buna-Monowitz. This was an industrial center and rubber factory (like many others, backed by billions in German investments) where prisoners worked as slave laborers.

Above the entrance to the main camp, a sign sculpted from metal greeted arriving prisoners: WORK MAKES YOU FREE. Of course, this was a lie. Working hard or doing a good job in no way meant that prisoners would be set free, or even live. Laborers were often worked literally to death. Thousands of deportees never even got the chance to work; they were killed immediately upon arrival in the gas chambers at Birkenau.

On May 4, 1942, the gassings at Auschwitz–Birkenau began. This highly efficient method of extermination would eventually kill 1.25 million people and make the name *Auschwitz* synonymous with "hell on earth." Until that point, most prisoners had come from Poland, where the highest concentration (3.3 million) of European Jews had lived before the war. But in the spring of 1942, deportation trains began running regularly from other parts of Europe. Filip Muller, a 20-year-old Czechoslovakian Jew, arrived at the camp on a Sunday in May:

> *. . . they herded us to [a] big room and told us to undress the corpses. I looked around me. There were hundreds of bodies, all dressed. Piled with the corpses were suitcases, [and] bundles. . . . I couldn't understand any of it. It was like a blow on the head, as if I'd been stunned. . . . I couldn't understand how they managed to kill so many people at once.*

Word Spreads

On the same day that the gassings began at Auschwitz–Birkenau, construction of Sobibór, another death camp in German-occupied Poland, was completed. Jews were rounded up by the thousands from ghettos throughout Poland and shipped to this new death center, northeast of Auschwitz. In the first month of Sobibór's operation, 19 deportations eliminated six Jewish communities entirely. The approximate populations of these communities are believed to be as follows:

- *May 6:* 2,500 from the Deblin ghetto
- *May 7:* 2,500 from the Ryki ghetto

- *May 8:* 3,500 from the Konskovola ghetto; 1,500 from the Baranov ghetto; 1,500 from the Polish village of Markuszov
- *May 9:* 800 from the Lobartov ghetto; 1,500 from the Markuszov ghetto

------------------------- Moments of Peace -------------------------

Every country in German-occupied Europe had a transit camp where Jews who had been rounded up by the Gestapo were sent to await deportation. As deportations increased in the spring of 1942, the transit camps began to fill at a faster rate than they had before the Wannsee Conference.

The main transit camp in Holland was Westerbork, outside the city of Amsterdam. It was here that teenage diarist Anne Frank and her family were sent when they were discovered in hiding. Helen and Siegfried Wohlfarth, who were discovered by the Gestapo in a suburb of Amsterdam, were also sent to Westerbork. Here they met thousands of Jewish prisoners. Helen later recalled that most of them were hoping to stay at this camp until the end of the war, but nearly all would eventually be deported. Many years after the war, Helen wrote about her arrival at Westerbork:

Jews arrive at the Westerbork transit camp, 1942.

Men and women were separated, children staying with their mothers. At tables in the barracks, families could take their meals together. I saw not a single German guard or soldier, only Jewish men and women in green uniforms called "camp police." The spirit was surprisingly high and hopeful, and we met some old friends with whom we had lost touch. . . .

In the early morning hours of September 3, our name was called over the barrack loudspeaker to report very early to the train station. . . . Some of the old friends came when they heard, and offered to bring us blankets and other items. . . . In three days the camp was emptied, with only 300 Jews allowed to remain.

That was just the beginning. Within 18 months, approximately 250,000 people had been murdered at Sobibór. Ber Moiseyevich Freiberg was one of only about 60 known survivors. Later, he said:

> *I witnessed scenes of frightfully inhuman treatment of innocent people. I saw a train arrive from Bialystok crammed full of completely naked people. . . . the half-dead on this train were mixed in with the dead. . . .*

Many of the world's ordinary citizens still did not fully know what was happening to Jews in Eastern Europe. Rumors had leaked out, but as yet there had been few reliable reports. In May, a Polish underground group called the Jewish Socialist Party, based in Warsaw, sent word to England of the killing of approximately 700,000 Jews in Galicia, a province in the east. The report stated:

> *. . . men, fourteen to sixty years old, were driven to a single place . . . where they were slaughtered or shot by machine-gun or killed by hand grenades. They had to dig their own graves. Children in orphanages, inmates in old-age homes, the sick in hospitals were shot, women were killed in the streets. In many towns the Jews were carried off to "an unknown destination" or killed in adjacent woods.*

The report told of mass killings at the Belzec death camp and made it clear that murder happened there on a regular basis. Still, no Allied government took any action to stop the massacre of the Jews of Europe.

Consequences of Defiance

Jews were not the only people to suffer at the hands of the Nazis. Hitler and his party sought to destroy anyone who did not support their ideas. In Berlin, on May 27, 1942, a group of 152 students parading with anti-Nazi posters was surrounded by police. All 152 were shot.

That same day, SS official Reinhard Heydrich was shot in Prague, Czechoslovakia, while riding in an open car, which was a brazen act in an occupied country. He died a week later; Heydrich was the only high-ranking Nazi to be killed during World War II. The "Blond Beast" had been targeted for death by Czech agents who parachuted into the country on order of the British government.

Heydrich's murder was very embarrassing to the Nazis, for it showed that their leaders were not indestructible. Even though no Jews had been involved, Nazi propaganda chief Josef Goebbels held them responsible:

> . . . *In any event we are holding the Jews to account. I am order-ing the arrest of 500 Berlin Jews which I had been planning, and I am informing the Jewish community leaders that for every Jewish assassination and for every attempt at revolt on the part of Jews, 100 or 150 Jews in our hands will be shot.*

An infuriated Adolf Hitler also sought revenge. He ordered increased deportations to Treblinka, Belzec, and Sobibór under the code name "Operation Reinhard." Certain Nazis, however, felt that a stronger *Aktion* was needed, for by then, the murder of Jews was commonplace. They wanted "a dramatic symbol which would show not only the Czechs but also all of Europe the con-sequences of defying German rule."

That "symbol" became the small Czech village of Lidice, where the Nazis thought the parachutists might have landed. The opera-tion began about 9:30 on the evening of June 9. Women and children were taken in one group, males over age 15 in another. Ten at a time, men were shot and buried in a mass grave by Jewish prisoners from Theresienstadt. Women and children were loaded onto trains for deportation. Then the entire village of Lidice was burned and its ashes were bulldozed. Not one trace of the community remained.

According to Gestapo figures, 199 men were murdered and 195 women were deported. Of nearly 100 children, only 16 could be found after the war.

"Why Do We Have to Suffer So?"

I hear a lot of noise and weeping. Now I already know that a poor man stole bread from a woman. . . . Further on I see a dead man lying in the street. He died of hunger, that's certain, like so many people in this war. . . . On my way home I meet lots more people in the streets begging the Germans for bread. All these scenes are very hard to bear and I go home sad. One question is in my mind: Why do we have to suffer so?

It was June 1942 when 14-year-old Kann made this entry in a diary while hiding in the Warsaw ghetto. Of the hundreds of ghettos scattered across Europe during the Nazi years, the most nightmarish was in Poland's capital, Warsaw.

The Warsaw Ghetto

Soon after the Nazis invaded Poland in September 1939, they began moving all Jews into ghettos. The largest of these was at Warsaw. Jewish workers were forced to build a brick wall around

----

A starving, homeless Jewish girl lies unconscious in a street of the Warsaw ghetto.

A food-rations card was issued each month to ghetto residents. This one allows four portions of meat, flour, jam, and sugar for the month of October 1942.

the ghetto to separate it from the rest of the city. By November 1940, the ghetto was sealed off from the outside world. At year's end, a total of 350,000 Jews were crowded into this 3½-square-mile (9-square-kilometer) living area.

With so many people crowded into such a small area, the ghetto quickly became filthy and disease-ridden. Reported Mary Berg, an outsider who visited one of the dwellings in the ghetto:

> *It is a desolate building. The former walls of the separate rooms have been broken down to form large halls; there are no conveniences; the plumbing has been destroyed. Near the walls are cots made of boards and covered with rags. . . . On the floor I saw half-naked, unwashed children lying listlessly.*

The *Judenrat*, or "Jewish Council," was in charge of keeping law and order in the ghetto. Council chairman Adam Czerniakow and 23 other prominent Jews appointed by the Nazis made up the council. It was the *Judenrat*'s job to carry out the Nazis' orders—establish police and labor forces, organize a food-rationing system, set up postal and medical facilities—and collect taxes, which went straight into German hands. Jews "volunteered" (under pressure from the Nazis) to be on the Council, but they were faced with an impossible dilemma. No matter what they did, they would be torn between the Nazis and the Jews. For their cooperation, *Judenrat* members were promised protection or special treatment for themselves or their families. Those rewards rarely materialized.

The Ghetto's Children

All residents of the ghetto suffered from hunger, bitter cold, and disease resulting from severe overcrowding. But ghetto life was hardest on the children. Warsaw ghetto historian Emanuel

Ringelblum, who buried his notes in milk cans discovered after the war, wrote, "The most fearful sight is that of freezing children [standing] dumbly weeping in the street with bare feet, bare knees, and torn clothing."

Survivor David Wdowinsky, who was a psychiatrist in a Warsaw hospital during the war, agreed: "Of all the gruesome scenes and sounds of the ghetto that remained with [me], the saddest and most haunting of all were. . . the children." Wdowinsky told of pedotrophy, a disease developed by ghetto children. Very rapidly, he recalled, the disease "aged infants into senility with hair sprouting from their wizened old faces."

The Germans built no schools for the 40,000 children in the Warsaw ghetto; Jews were forbidden to attend school. Ghetto residents, however, were determined that their children would not go uneducated. Adults set up schools in the ghetto that were disguised as workshops, like shoe-repair or tailor shops. G. Silkes recalled one such school:

There would be five or six people in a room with a teacher. . . . And there were no books. Because suddenly if the Germans came breaking in, the children would give the teacher shoes and he became a shoe-maker, or a piece of cloth and he was suddenly a tailor.

Children who were caught smuggling goods into the Warsaw ghetto are detained by the authorities.

Because they were small, children were very important in smuggling supplies such as food, medicine, soap, and electrical appliances into the ghetto. Those smugglers who were caught were arrested or shot on the spot—even children. Still, the ghetto's youngest residents continued to try, for they knew that they had little to lose. Dressed in clothes that were several sizes too large for them, the young smugglers would stand at the ghetto gates to pass or receive the goods, which they quickly hid beneath the folds of their clothing. Some slipped through cracks in the ghetto walls or between bars on the gates. Others crawled through sewer pipes to the outside.

The death rate among Warsaw ghetto children was very high. Many were tortured or shot. "Natural" deaths—that is, deaths in the ghetto resulting primarily from starvation and disease, rather than from shootings or beatings—totaled approximately 85,000. Of these, some 20,000 were children. Mary Berg, who recorded daily life in *Warsaw Ghetto: A Diary*, wrote:

> *There are a great number of almost naked children whose parents have died, and who sit in rags on the streets. Their bodies are horribly emaciated. . . . They no longer have a human appearance and are more like monkeys than children. They no longer beg for bread, but for death. . . .*

"Resettlement to the East"

Throughout the spring of 1942, rumors ran through the ghetto of a German plan to "resettle" Jews farther east in Poland. On April 29, Adam Czerniakow was ordered by the Nazis to supply population figures, street by street and building by building. In early July, when 110 Jews were shot to death on the streets, rumors of large-scale deportations became intense. Some said that as many as 60,000 to 70,000 Jews were going to be resettled—that is, shipped to death and labor camps.

Although the Gestapo called the rumors "rubbish," on July 22, 1942, at 7:30 A.M., German police surrounded the ghetto. The *Judenrat* was given instructions that all Warsaw Jews were to be resettled in the east. Each person was to take only seven pounds (15 kilograms) of personal belongings, all valuables, and enough food and water to last for three days.

Adam Czerniakow: "I Am Powerless . . ."

What Adam Czerniakow, chairman of the *Judenrat* ("Jewish Council") in the Warsaw ghetto, did on July 23, 1942, was the subject of great debate among Jews. Throughout the spring and summer of 1942, the Nazis demanded more and more Jews for "resettlement to the east." It was Czerniakow's job to supply them. Families begged and pleaded with him to spare their loved ones, and Czerniakow bargained with the Nazis. But it was to no avail.

By July 22, the Germans were demanding 6,000 Jews a day. "When I asked for the number of days per week in which the operation would be carried out, the number was seven days a week," Czerniakow wrote in his diary. "The SS wants me to kill children with my own hands. This I cannot do."

Frantically, Czerniakow negotiated with the Nazis, trying to save as many people as he could. By the morning of July 23, he had been able to arrange deals for some—but not for his wife nor for the orphans in the ghetto. Devastated and depressed, he wrote notes to his wife and coworkers. "I am powerless...," he confessed. "My heart trembles in sorrow and compassion. I can no longer bear all this. My act will prove to everyone what is the right thing to do." And with that, Adam Czerniakow swallowed a cyanide pill.

Some people called Czerniakow a hero for committing suicide. They felt that killing himself was an act of courage that showed strength and defiance. But others, among them ghetto historian Emanuel Ringelblum, saw Czerniakow's suicide as cowardly. "...Too late, a sign of weakness," wrote Ringelblum. "...[He] should have called for resistance—a weak man."

The deportations were carried out swiftly and in large numbers. Working street by street through the ghetto, the Nazis sent approximately 6,000 to 9,000 people per day to the death camps. The deportees were herded together at the transit point, where they awaited shipment on cattle cars that had no windows, heating or cooling, toilets, food, or water. After the first weeks of deportations, more than 66,700 Jews were removed from the Warsaw ghetto and killed.

Treblinka

The destination for most Warsaw residents was the Treblinka death camp, a killing center that opened on July 23, 1942. Treblinka was the last of the three extermination camps built along Poland's Bug River. It was also the largest and most efficient death center built to date. Like the other Bug River killing centers, the purpose of Treblinka was kept very secret.

There were two camps at Treblinka. Camp I had stores, workshops, and even a courtyard, supposedly where concerts and athletic events would be held. But it was all fake, built to keep prisoners from realizing they were actually in a death camp. If prisoners really knew their fate, the Nazis reasoned, they would panic and cause problems. The sole purpose of Treblinka's Camp II was to kill people, and to kill them quickly. The only residents of the camp were the squads of Jews whose jobs were to burn and bury the bodies.

From July 1942 until October of that year, three-fourths of Warsaw's Jews were murdered at Treblinka. The death factory eventually used 13 carbon-monoxide chambers. Approximately 50,000 people were killed at Treblinka per month.

Resistance

Angered by the Warsaw deportations, Jews began organizing a resistance movement within days of the first trains leaving. Resisters wanted to warn people about their fates, with what little information was available, and to plan resistance activities. The group was known as ZOB, from the Polish words meaning the "Jewish Fighters Organization." Most resistance fighters were young, in their teens and early 20s. Members had no military training and few guns. They did, however, have a fierce determination.

Inside the ghetto, the ZOB built underground rooms and passageways. They put sandbags near the windows and prepared themselves for warfare. Women and girls whose hair color and facial features did not resemble what the Nazis identified as "Jewish" would sneak outside the ghetto to make deals on guns and ammunition. If the Germans were aware of what was going on, they seemed to think that the ZOB posed little threat. They would soon be proven wrong.

A kind of spiritual resistance was organized by a doctor and educator named Janusz Korczak, who ran an orphanage in the Warsaw ghetto.

On August 6, the Nazis announced that children's groups were the next to be resettled. Korczak suspected that this meant death at Treblinka. Calmly, lest the children panic, he lined them up parade-style:

Yitzak Zuckerman and his wife Tzvia Lubetkin were two of the founders and leaders of the ZOB resistance organization.

The orphans were clutching flasks of water and their favorite books and toys. One hundred and ninety-two children and ten adults were counted off by the Nazis. Korczak stood at the head of his wards, a child holding each hand. . . . They marched through the ghetto to the Umschlagplatz *[transit point], where they joined thousands of people waiting in the broiling August sun.*

Janusz Korczak went to his death with the orphans at Treblinka. Said one witness who watched them board the train: "This was no march to the train cars, but rather a mute protest against the murderous regime. . . a process the like of which no human eye had ever witnessed."

But the Germans were by no means through, for more than 115,000 people remained in the Warsaw ghetto. On September 5, the Nazis ordered ghetto residents to report for registration and to bring food for two days. This was the start of another deportation that would last a week, with literally thousands of Jews being shipped out each day. By September 13, approximately 300,000 Warsaw ghetto Jews had been deported and murdered.

"I Have a Number in My Skin Now"

She takes my arm and slowly the blue pen's point sinks into my skin. It burns a little. I watch. A number starts to show from under my skin. It was not there before. I have a number in my skin now. I walk away holding my arm with the other hand, and read again: B-4828. . . .

Identifying the Condemned

In the Auschwitz labor camp, tattooing was actually a sign of hope. Prisoners who were tattooed with a number were being "spared" to work for the Reich. They would not be sent immediately to the gas chambers. "In Auschwitz," recalled survivor Carol Frenkel Lipson, "a number meant life. . . . We knew if we didn't get a number, we were destined for the crematorium [oven]." Most children under 14 were never tattooed. The Nazis considered them too small and weak to work as slave laborers. Those children were usually killed upon arrival.

Dutch Jews selected for forced labor in a quarry line up at Buchenwald concentration camp.

Tattooing was the system used to identify prisoners at Auschwitz, but Jews in the outside world also had to wear special symbols to identify themselves. These were yellow stars, sewn to clothing, representing the Star of David, a Jewish symbol. This system had been in effect in Germany since 1940. On April 29, 1942, it became required in Holland, and soon after in Belgium, both occupied by the Germans. On June 7, Jews in German-occupied France were also required to wear the Star.

Self-Preservation

Nine-year-old Lalka was a Polish Jew whose parents had disappeared at the hands of the Nazis. For a time, she and her older brother, Benyek, and their six-year-old brother, Olek, lived alone in a ghetto. They begged and stole what food they could, trying desperately to stay alive. When Benyek decided to run away, Lalka and Olek were left on their own. Eventually, the Nazis rounded them up for deportation and herded them into a railroad boxcar, where they were told to take off their clothes. Later, Lalka described what happened:

> *Suddenly someone pushed Olek. He fell. . . . Olek yelled. He called my name. I immediately attacked the man, biting him and beating him with my fists.*
>
> *. . . The car was full of naked, crawling bodies. I bit and scratched my way through, trying to defend myself. . . . I suddenly spied a little foot sticking out of a pile of bodies. It was wearing a familiar sock, my little brother's sock!*
>
> *. . . [At last] I managed to get him out from under all those bodies. . . . He looked as if he were asleep, his mouth wide open, but I couldn't wake him. I fiercely embraced his body, clasping him to my chest. I screamed, without making a sound. I cried, without shedding a tear.*

It was not unusual that no one tried to help Lalka and her brother. To the Jews destined for deportation, life had become a matter of simple self-preservation. There was little opportunity or ability to help others or to share bread or water. In such harsh conditions, it was often each person for himself.

For those trying to survive on the streets, life was hardly better. Most Jews had no means for helping each other, and most sympathetic Gentiles were too afraid to try. Punishments for aiding

Bergen-Belsen: Typhus Graveyard

Late in 1942, Heinrich Himmler began making plans for what would become one of the Nazis' most notorious concentration camps. Bergen-Belsen, near Hannover, Germany, was planned as a model "camp" where teams from the Red Cross and other international aid organizations could come to inspect the treatment of prisoners. But as more victims arrived, starvation increased and the camp became a massive infectious-disease center. Thousands died of typhus and tuberculosis.

The daily horror of Bergen-Belsen was difficult for adults or strong-willed teenagers to comprehend, but it was nearly impossible for children. Laszlo and Eva, five and eight years old, were shipped to Bergen-Belsen with their mother. There, Eva witnessed scenes that would forever change her life. After only days in the camp, she no longer thought of corpses as once-living human beings; they were simply shriveled hulks. Scenes around her no longer shocked her senses. She became incapable of screaming or crying, no matter how awful the sight.

Every day, Eva did as her mother told her. She cared for her brother who had typhus, and she believed her mother when she said that "this" would not last much longer. Then one day, Eva's mother, who had also contracted typhus, became too sick to move. Eva was unable to offer her anything—even fresh water—to ease her suffering. All the child could do was hold her mother in her arms while she died.

Among the other helpless victims of this monstrous typhus graveyard were 15-year-old Anne Frank and her older sister, Margot. They had been shipped to Bergen-Belsen from Auschwitz, where their mother, Edith, had died. Shortly after New Year's Day in 1945, Margot, who was very ill, fell out of her bunk. She had become so weak by that point that, when she hit the floor, she died from the shock of the impact. A few days later, on January 6—just three months before she might have been liberated—Anne died of typhus. Her father, Otto, and Anne's now-famous diary were the only remnants of the family to survive.

Children at the Polish ghetto of Lodz search the ground for food or fuel.

and harboring Jews had become so severe that many Gentiles were unwilling to take the risk.

Not every country was unwilling to take a stand, however. Sweden, a neutral country, offered protection to Dutch Jews who could get themselves over the borders. But the Nazis responded by depriving the Jews of their citizenship; without the proper papers, they had little chance of being allowed into any country. The Belgian government and its citizens made the same offer to Belgian Jews, taking approximately 25,000 into their homes despite enormous risks. Most in this group were saved, but a similar number were deported—and, of that group, fewer than 1,300 lived to the end of the war.

Killings Increase

After the Wannsee Conference, the number of deportations, mass murders, and killings in the streets increased steadily across Europe. In German-occupied Riga, Latvia, on June 9, a gas van was brought in to murder the thousands of Jews right in that ghetto. When the leaders of this *Aktion* realized what a massive job lay before them, they requested a second killing van.

Even though they were less efficient than the gas chambers, the vans were still an effective tool of death for the Nazis. Adolf

Eichmann's Department of Jewish Affairs reported that, in six months, more than 97,000 people had been murdered in vans. It was clear that the vans were being used nearly around the clock.

Suspecting death in the near future, a group of 2,000 Jews from the Dzisna ghetto in a German-occupied part of the Soviet Union planned an escape. Some were caught, but most managed to find safety within a Soviet partisan group. The Jews living near Nieswiez, to the south, were not so fortunate. Of the 600 artists, musicians, and writers there, most were killed when they tried to revolt with sticks and clubs.

In Cracow, Poland, well-known Jewish figures became victims of persecution. Mordechai Gebirtig was one. He was a 65-year-old carpenter who composed and sang songs in Yiddish. Many of his songs encouraged Jews to be happy, despite the savagery of the Nazis. In one of his ballads, he reminded them that a good sense of humor would keep them strong:

> *Jews . . . don't walk about in sadness, but be patient and have faith. . . .*
> *Don't relinquish for a moment your weapon of laughter and gaiety, for it keeps you united.*

In June, Gebirtig was arrested by the Gestapo and shipped to the Belzec death camp. The same month, 70-year-old writer Abraham Naumann was shot and killed during a street round-up of Cracow Jews. They were just two of thousands.

A Major *Aktion*

By early July 1942, nearly 250,000 of the 3.3 million Jews in German-occupied Poland had been killed. But even this was not enough for SS chief Heinrich Himmler. On July 19, Himmler announced that the ghettos of Eastern Europe were to be emptied by the end of the year. He said that this needed to be done ". . . in the interest of the security and cleanliness of the German Reich and its sphere of interest." By removing the Jews, Himmler said he hoped to eliminate "a source of moral and physical pestilence [disease]," adding that a "total cleansing is necessary and therefore to be carried out." Three days later, liquidation of the Warsaw ghetto was accelerated.

In Western Europe, the 140,000 Jews of Holland had been persecuted far less than Jews in Eastern Europe, but in July, that changed. Thousands of Dutch Jews were arrested and scheduled for deportation—many of them from the Amsterdam ghetto. The next day, the first train, carrying some 1,135 victims, left for a destination unknown to its passengers but well known to the Nazis: Auschwitz–Birkenau. By month's end, more than 6,000 other Dutch Jews had suffered the same fate. Most were murdered upon arrival.

By August 1942, the number of innocent people being rounded up for extermination climbed to even more staggering heights. In the first two weeks of the month, a quarter-million Jews were killed at Birkenau, by death squads in the east, or at the three death camps along the Bug River. Sometimes, a town's entire population was wiped out in a single *Aktion*. In the Volhynia region of German-occupied Poland, approximately 87,000 Jews were murdered. Some 15,000 escaped into the forests but were unable to survive the next two years of starvation, cold, and illness. Only 1,000 lived to war's end. Before the end of the year, more than 140,000 Jews from Volhynia were dead, along with 300,000 non-Jewish Poles who had also tried to resist the Nazis.

Lvov

In the Lvov ghetto, the SS began a roundup on August 10, 1942. It lasted most of the month. During that time, 40,000 Jews were deported to Belzec and murdered. Those too weak to work— which included children, the elderly, and the ill—became special targets. But even able-bodied Jews were shipped to their deaths when there was available space on a train.

David Kahane was among the Jews of Lvov who tried to save himself and his family, particularly his three-year-old daughter.

At 3:00 A.M. on August 17,
Kahane was awakened by the
yelling of SS officers in the
street below his apartment. He
awoke, dressed his daughter,
and tried to get her to safety.
When she started to cry,
Kahane panicked, "fearing her
cry could be heard outside,"
and he spanked the youngster.
Later, he painfully recalled that
moment:

> *. . . I have never been able to
> forgive myself for slapping,
> even lightly, my little innocent
> lamb. I am sure I was not the
> only father to lose his temper
> that morning. Everywhere con-
> fused fathers stood helpless with
> their little children . . . asking
> one and the same question:
> "What shall I do? Where can
> we hide?"*

Victims of brutality hang in the Lvov market square, 1942.

Kahane and his family survived, thanks to the help of Gentiles
who found hiding places for them. Others were not so fortunate.
On August 26, in the town of Kielce, a young man and his mother were among the more than 20,000 Jews scheduled for deportation to Treblinka. Abraham Jacob Krzepicki, a survivor, recalled
what happened to the pair when they arrived at the camp:

> *When it came time to separate them—women to the left and men
> to the right—the son wanted to say a last goodbye to his mother.
> When [the guard] tried to drive him away, he took out a pocket-
> knife and stuck it into [him]. As a punishment, they [the SS] spent
> all that day shooting all the Jews from Kielce who were at the camp.*

"It Is the Silence That Frightens Me"

In September 1932, Frajdla Leiber was born in the village the Poles called Oświecim. Adolf Hitler was not yet in power, the Germans had not yet invaded Poland, and the Nazis had not yet built a death camp in Frajdla's hometown.

Shortly after her birth, the Leibers left Poland for Paris, France, where Frajdla spent her childhood. Ten years later, she returned, but not for a pleasant homecoming. Frajdla was among the Jews captured in German-occupied Paris. She was deported to her hometown, which the German regime called Auschwitz. There, she became one of the thousands gassed to death in Auschwitz–Birkenau during the stepped-up campaign ordered by Heinrich Himmler.

Death in Poland

Auschwitz–Birkenau was a frequent destination for Jews from Western Europe, as it was geographically closest to them. During September, eight trains departed from Holland, five from Belgium,

----
Inmates work at forced labor in the infamous Mauthausen quarry. Prisoners were worked to exhaustion and given no protection from wind, rain, or snow.

and 13 from Paris, France—all headed to the infamous camps in German-occupied Poland. A Jewish girl named Helene was the eldest of three children living in Paris in 1942, when the Nazis intensified their deportation program. Caught up in the sweep were her parents, her maternal grandparents, and her younger brother. Helene was never able to say goodbye to them—and it has haunted her ever since. Even decades after the war, she said, "I've never been able to talk about. . . all that. The words get stuck in the back of my throat."

Auschwitz–Birkenau was only one of many destinations for deportees. In the Polish village of Dzialoszyce, more than 9,000 Jews were scheduled for Belzec on September 3. Before the trains were loaded, however, the SS simply shot some 1,000 victims in the streets. A handful of Dzialoszyce's Jews managed to escape and form partisan units, but within three months, they, too, had been hunted down and executed. Nine trainloads—approximately 14,000 people—were sent from towns in Ukraine and Poland to Belzec on September 7.

The killing of 1942 continued in huge numbers, all across Europe, every single day and night:

- *September 10:* More than 530 Jews are deported from Nuremberg, Germany. Only 27 of all Nuremberg's Jews survive the war. The same day, approximately 13,000 Jews from two different regions of Poland are shipped to Belzec.

- *September 21:* On Yom Kippur, the holiest day to Jews, killings and deportations are scheduled all over Europe. Nearly 30,000 people are shot or sent to the extermination camp. Another 10,000 are removed from the Terezin ghetto to an area of White Russia (present-day Belarus). Of those 10,000, wrote Nazi hunter Simon Wiesenthal, "Nobody knows of any survivors."

- *September 23:* Over the next week, some 16,000 Jews from Lodz, Poland, are murdered at Chelmno.

These were not the only killings on these days, nor were these the only days of killing. Across the German-controlled lands, hundreds of thousands of people were murdered every day.

As early as 1938, the United States and other world powers were well informed about the persecution of the Jews in Germany. Newspapers ran articles on the plight of the Jews, so the general public also had some knowledge of growing antisemitic events in Europe.

On July 6, 1938, ambassadors from 32 countries met in the town of Evian, France, to discuss the Jewish refugee problem. Some of the smaller countries, such as Denmark and Holland, opened their doors to the Jews, even though these nations were already crowded with refugees. Many countries, though, followed the unfortunate lead of Australia, whose representative announced at the meeting, "As we have no real racial problem, we are not desirous of importing one."

In the United States, Americans were still recovering from the Great Depression. Jobs were scarce and money was tight. Many people believed that allowing more immigrants into the country would take the few remaining jobs away from American citizens. As a result, the United States made no changes in its immigration laws to allow more Jews to emigrate.

After the United States entered World War II in 1941, reports of atrocities against the Jews increased. But despite the reports, the American people seemed to care little about the plight of "foreigners" on another continent. The news media played down the reports, and the government took no action. American Jewish groups held rallies to protest the apathy, but still nothing was done.

On August 8, 1942, the World Jewish Congress in Switzerland sent a cable to Rabbi Stephen S. Wise, president of the group in the United States. It described a reported plan

. . . to exterminate all Jews from. . . German controlled areas in Europe after they have been concentrated in the east. The number involved is said to be between three and a half and four million, and the object to permanently settle the Jewish question in Europe.

The cable was never delivered to Rabbi Wise. It was held up by people in the U.S. government who said that they wanted to confirm the source. Yet, even when the source was confirmed, the government took no action. Finally, in January 1944, Secretary of the Treasury Henry Morgenthau protested to President Franklin D. Roosevelt. Something must be done, he demanded. The president established the War Refugee Board to help rescue Europe's Jews. But, admitted one board member, "What we did was . . . late and little, I would say."

Before these people were murdered, they were first robbed. The Nazis forced prisoners to give up all their possessions.

The Nazis also confiscated mountains of household items, such as scissors, nail files, toothbrushes, combs, silverware, kitchen utensils, even artificial arms and legs and children's dolls and toys. As historian Michael Berenbaum explained:

> Deportees arrived at Auschwitz and Birkenau expecting resettlement elsewhere, so it was natural for them to bring along articles of daily living. . . . But these were false expectations, encouraged by Nazi deceptions. SS guards immediately confiscated the belongings of all newcomers.

Death by Labor

Not all deportees were shipped to extermination camps. Thousands were deported to slave labor camps where, if they did not die of exhaustion, starvation, or disease, they were very often shot. Conditions in these camps were terrible. Inmates were expected to work 10- to 12-hour shifts with few or no breaks. They were fed a diet of thin, watery soup or dry black bread, and were surrounded by filth, disease, and grossly inadequate sanitary facilities. Lice crawled through the barracks and across their bodies, spreading typhus and other fatal diseases.

One of the worst labor camps was Mauthausen in annexed Austria, the site of a huge stone quarry. There, the weak and starving inmates slaved 11 hours a day, hauling huge blocks of stone on their shoulders 186 steps up the side of the quarry. When they got their burdens to the top they might be beaten, shot, or pushed into the quarry below.

Local Austrians were not blind to the goings-on in Mauthausen and its sub-camps. Wrote historian Konnilyn Feig:

> When the prisoners arrived at the small railroad station, the village children waited to throw stones at them as they began their march to the camp. The villagers also taunted them as they got off the

*train, "You'll soon be up the chimney on Totenburg" [where the
crematorium was located].*

Austria—in particular its capital of Vienna—had long been a
hotbed of antisemitism. It was there that Adolf Hitler, an Austrian
by birth, developed his hatred of Jews. Hitler said that, in
Vienna, where he lived as a young man, his

*eyes were opened to two menaces . . . whose terrible importance
for the existence of the German people I did not understand:
Marxism [a socialist belief] and Jewry.*

In Vienna, he also learned about the *volkisch*, or "people's,"
movement, led by a group of fanatic Germans who felt the world
was being threatened by foreigners, particularly Jews. Those in
the *volkisch* movement believed fiercely in the superiority of the
"Germanic" people—and the inferiority of the Jews.

Since the 1938 *Anschluss* or "reunification of the Germanic
people," when Germany took over Austria without protest from
the Austrian citizens, Austrians had supported Hitler's beliefs.
Neither the government nor its citizens did much to protect
Austria's approximately 185,000 Jews. Throughout the war,
Austrians continued to ignore the fate of the Jews, both out of
fear for their own lives and families, and because so many of
them were strong anti-Semites. Those who were concerned did
little to help.

In 1942, Anna Strasser, an Austrian Gentile, was sent to work
in the accounting office at camp St. Valentin, near the infamous
Mauthausen quarry. After some weeks, what she witnessed
began to weigh heavily on her. From the windows of her office,
she saw

*. . . that the inmates were beaten to death. . . . One absolutely lost
one's wits. . . . I simply could no longer endure this great burden.
So one day I broke down. I cried and cried. For many weeks I was
registered sick.*

Johann Steinmuller, a local stoneworker, was hired by the SS to train inmates to break paving stones. When he saw the conditions they endured, Steinmuller was appalled and tried to help.

> *During stone-breaking an inmate sank backward and asked for water. I went to an* Untersturmführer *[SS official at the camp] whose name I do not know, and requested that I be given water for the inmate. . . . It was pointed out to me that I was an impossible person, that you just don't do that, [ask] that water be given out for the inmates, etc. . . . An hour later I was immediately dismissed.*

Many of the slave-labor camps were small, but conditions were just as horrible as at the larger camps. Teenagers stood a slightly better chance of survival because they were young, healthy, and strong when they came in. Hirsh Altusky later described what it was like working on a hydraulic press at a camp in German-occupied Poland:

> *The chemical used was green and poisonous. [Soon] we were covered with it, and you couldn't wash it off. Even our closest friends avoided us like lepers. We worked from six in the morning until six at night. People died standing at the machines. There were explosions. At this work you could not survive more than four, maybe six weeks.*

Into Hiding

By the autumn of 1942, the "underground" resistance movement in many German-occupied countries was successfully helping Jews to find hiding places. It was extremely dangerous to go into hiding, both for the victims and for their protectors. A family caught hiding a Jew usually suffered the same fate as the Jew: deportation to a concentration camp or death camp.

The most famous family to go into hiding was that of Otto Frank, whose daughter Anne kept a diary. Anne's diary ran from June 1942, when preparations for hiding were being made, until August 1944, when she and her family were discovered in

Amsterdam, Holland, by the Gestapo. On one of her first days hiding in her father's warehouse—her "Secret Annex"—Anne confided to her diary:

> *It is the silence that frightens me so in the evenings and at night. . . . I can't tell you how oppressive it is never to be able to go outdoors, also I'm very afraid that we shall be discovered and be shot. . . . We have to whisper and tread lightly during the day, otherwise the people in the warehouse might hear us. . . .*

Another family to go into hiding were the Wohlfarths. Their four-year-old daughter, Doris, however, posed a problem. It was very difficult to take a young child into hiding. Living space was tight, food was scarce, and, as Anne Frank said in her diary, one had to be quiet much of the time. A safer course was to place the child in a Gentile home. Through Jo Vis, a friend in the underground, the Wohlfarths found a family willing to take Doris. Wrote Helen:

Anne Frank recorded much of her experience in hiding on the pages of her now-famous diary. Anne and her sister Margot died in Bergen-Belsen in 1945.

> *The next two nights, Jo came to transport Doris's clothing, her bed and many of her toys. Even her doll house was waiting for her at her new home. . . .*

It would have been too dangerous for Helen and Siegfried to know the names of Doris's new family. If ever they were caught, the Gestapo would pressure them for information about their children, and it would be better if they did not know where Doris was living. It was a Sunday afternoon when Doris's new parents arrived to take her away:

> *After a short visit, the five of us walked to the nearest streetcar stop. We said goodbye as casually as possible and gave those strangers our child. This was October 22, six days before Doris's fifth birthday, the last time her father ever saw her.*

"A Spiritual Prison"

The Holocaust, when spelled with a capital *H*, refers to the planned destruction of the Jews of Europe by the Nazis. With the exception of the Romani (Gypsies), no other entire group was singled out for genocide. However, many other so-called "enemies of the Reich" were targeted for torture and extermination. Among them were Jehovah's Witnesses, Austrian and German male homosexuals, the mentally and physically handicapped, Poles, Soviet prisoners of war, and members of various political groups. The difference between the Jews and the "others" was that Hitler did not plan to murder every single member of these other groups. Even the Romani, though targeted for death, were not the subjects of such intense personal hatred as were the Jews.

Residents of Lvov, Poland, stand in the street in front of a destroyed synagogue.

Purge in Poland

"Every nation under enemy occupation during World War II experienced a reign of terror by the Nazis," wrote historian Richard Lukas. "But no nation suffered more than Poland." From the moment German armies invaded in 1939, the Poles were treated brutally.

For centuries, German leaders had been hostile toward Poles, viewing them as inferior. Under Hitler, the Nazis sought what they called *Lebensraum*, "living space," for their growing "master race" of "Aryan" people—blond-haired, blue-eyed Germans who were supposedly "perfect" in every way. Poland was Hitler's choice for acquiring *Lebensraum*.

In December 1942, more than 40,000 Poles were expelled from their homeland. During this purge, the Nazis overtook 100 Polish villages where many of the residents were Gentiles. The fates of these people included murder in the streets, torture, and a variety of slave labor details in the concentration camps and elsewhere.

On January 23, 1943, the head of the Polish Home Army, General Stefan Rowecki, told government authorities, "A new wave of terror embraces the entire country." There were increased deportations to the camps and ongoing massacres in the streets. Said one official, referring to the 1942 massacre of nearly 500 innocent civilians in Lidice, Czechoslovakia, after the death of high-ranking Nazi Reinhard Heydrich, "We have thousands of Lidices in Poland."

Why didn't Polish Jews and Gentiles unite against their common enemy? A long Polish tradition of strong antisemitism meant that, although the Poles hated German occupation, they were not against the elimination of Jews from Poland. Indeed, pogroms—organized mob attacks—had taken place in Poland against Polish Jews at various times for centuries. This long-standing hatred was supported by the Polish government in the years before World War II. Simon Wiesenthal, a concentration-camp survivor who has spent the rest of his life tracking down Nazis, experienced the

Poles' hatred of Jews first-hand. In *The Wiesenthal File*, he had this to say about the Poles:

> . . . *they did not like us Jews—and that was no new thing.* . . . *A wise man once said that the Jews were the salt of the earth. But the Poles thought their land had been ruined by over-salting. Compared with Jews in other countries, therefore, we were maybe better prepared for what the Nazis had in store for us.* . . .

Polish citizens who did try to help the Jews were equally powerless against the Nazis; neither group could do much to help the other. But a number of Poles did try. One of the last books written by Warsaw ghetto historian Emanuel Ringelblum before his murder concerned Polish–Jewish relations. He cited many examples of his own experience of Gentile Poles who helped Jews hide or escape:

> *[Poles] who saved Jews at the risk of their lives and with boundless self-sacrifice—there are thousands such in Warsaw and the whole country. The names of these people* . . . *will forever remain engraved in our memories, the names of heroes who saved thousands of human beings from destruction in the fight against the greatest enemy of the human race.*

Non-Jewish Victims

The Romani, a people who lived primarily in Eastern Europe, were considered by the Nazis to be "subhumans." Excellent musicians and dancers who liked to wear colorful clothing and jewelry, the Romani usually made their money through fortune-telling, animal care, and metalworking. They claimed no citizenship and referred to themselves as *Rom*, which means "man." They lived in small groups that moved frequently and stayed away from government authorities, largely because, for centuries, they had been a despised minority in society. No one knows exactly how many Romani lived in Europe before World War II. Of the estimated

Prisoners in ghettos and Nazi concentration camps were identified by symbols sewn to their clothing. The symbols were cloth triangles sewn on the left side of the breast of their striped prisoners' uniforms.

The triangles were of different colors to identify each type of prisoner. Jehovah's Witnesses and others whose religious beliefs prevented them from joining the military wore purple. Germans with long and recurring prison records had green triangles. Red was for political prisoners, and black

was for "asocials"—those who, for various reasons, did not get along well in society. Homosexuals wore pink.

When the prisoners were first required to wear the cloth symbols, Jews were put into one of the above groups. They were required to wear the colored triangle of that group sewn over a yellow triangle, to form the six-pointed Star of David. This symbol of Judaism was to show the Germans that these prisoners were also Jewish. Later, they were required to wear a full yellow star sewn to all of their clothing.

700,000 Romani in Europe, perhaps as many as one-third—nearly a quarter-million people—died at the hands of the Nazis.

On December 16, 1942, the Germans announced a decree against the Romani. It meant that approximately 19,000 Romani would be gassed to death in August 1943.

Maria Sava Moise, a Romani, had been born in Romania. When she was 17, the people of her region were rounded up by police and deported in cattle cars to the Ukraine. "When we disembarked," Maria recalled, "we were marched to a farm and left in open fields to die slowly. That's how my sister died." Maria might have suffered the same fate had her father not been serving in the Romanian Army. By coincidence, his unit was stationed near the field where Maria had been left to die. On New Year's Day of 1943, he was able to smuggle her onto a troop train that carried her back to Romania.

Despite their persecution by the Nazis, Romani rarely resisted or fought back. Some considered it more heroic to die quietly, without a fight. Recalled Belgian writer Jan Yoors, who lived with the Romani during the war:

Living under the constant threat of sudden death, some of the older Rom remained unaffected by the appeal of violence; some said that it was perhaps better to let oneself be crucified than to demean oneself by crucifying others.

In addition to Jews, Gentile Poles, and Romani, perhaps as many as 5,000 German male homosexuals were murdered by the Nazis. (But despite Hitler's hatred of these people, one of the earliest members of the Nazi Party—Ernst Rohm—was himself openly homosexual. So were several other party members.) The mentally and physically handicapped—whom the Nazis called "useless eaters"—were killed by the tens of thousands. And an estimated 3 million Soviet prisoners of war were also murdered by the Nazis. These soldiers were "shot or starved to death long after they had been captured and disarmed."

Jehovah's Witnesses, a Christian group that refused to place the Nazis above God, were rounded up and shipped to labor camps. They were told that they would be freed if they rejected their faith, but few, if any, did. They preferred to stay, pray, and try to convert other inmates. As a result, perhaps as many as 20,000 Jehovah's Witnesses in the German-occupied countries perished in concentration camps.

The "White Rose"

Here and there across Europe, small groups of Gentiles gathered to speak out against Nazi persecution. At the University of Munich in Germany, Hans Scholl, his sister Sophie, and their friend Christopher Probst operated as the "White Rose." Together, they printed thousands of leaflets, mailing them, passing them out on the streets, dropping them out of windows onto side-walks. Their purpose, said White Rose, was to "strive for the renewal of the mortally wounded German spirit." By allowing

A "False Doctrine"

One of the reasons why Adolf Hitler and the Nazis so despised Jehovah's Witnesses was because they refused to show allegiance or support to any power other than God. According to their beliefs, they do not acknowledge political or military leaders. Jehovah's Witnesses are pacifists: They do not believe in war and will not bear arms or fight. In addition to refusing military service, they do not salute the flag of any country, say pledges of allegiance, run for public office, or vote in elections.

Since the religion was founded in the early 1870s, the Witnesses' beliefs have caused them problems with the governments of the countries where they live, but nowhere more than in Nazi Germany. In 1942, there were approximately 106,000 Jehovah's Witnesses worldwide, most of them living in the United States and Europe. Witnesses who lived in the German-occupied countries were subjected to harassment and persecution and sent to concentration camps for their refusal to pay homage to Adolf Hitler. Unlike the Jews, they were not the target of genocide, but as many as 6,000 of them were victims of the camps.

Nazis made Witnesses sign pledges stating that their religion was based on "a false doctrine" and verifying that they had "totally rejected this organization and freed [themselves] from the sect." The pledge further stated that those who signed it would "observe the laws of the nation especially in the event of war when [they would] take up arms to defend. . . the Fatherland." The last line informed signers that they could "expect a further term of protective custody" if they failed to adhere to the pledge.

Thousands of Witnesses did refuse the pledge and found themselves in the "protective custody" of concentration camps. They were respected by many of their fellow inmates in the camps for the way they faced death: willingly and without fear, almost happily, some reported, believing that they were giving their lives in service to God.

---

the evil Nazi regime to take over their country, the German people were "guilty, guilty, guilty!" the flyers declared. They had put themselves in a "spiritual prison."

The White Rose trio, who had been enthusiastic child members of the Hitler Youth, now encouraged the German people to resist the Nazis in any way they could—from refusing to obey orders to planning and carrying out acts of protest.

It did not take the Nazis long to respond to the defiance of the White Rose. Hans, Sophie, and Christopher—all in their early

20s—were tried in a "People's Court," found to be criminals, and sentenced to die. On February 22, 1943, they were beheaded. Hans's last words before his death were, "Long live freedom!"

Defiance Grows Stronger

In Bulgaria, defiance came from a totally unexpected source. In March 1943, the Bulgarian government, which until then had supported Germany and its Axis partners, was ordered by the Nazis to begin deportation of its Jews.

Hans Scholl (second from left) and his sister Sophie (on fence) were two of the three German Gentiles who operated as the "White Rose."

Before people realized what was happening, nearly 11,400 Jews from the Bulgarian regions of Macedonia and Thrace had been shipped to Treblinka and other death camps.

When citizen-based protests and pressure on the Bulgarian government grew too strong, Bulgaria refused to deport any more. Despite pressure from its Axis partners, Bulgarian leaders resisted, and in the end, its approximately 50,000 Jews were spared. Thus, Bulgaria became the only country under Nazi influence whose Jewish population did not dwindle during the war.

As life in the ghettos grew increasingly grim, the resistance movement grew increasingly strong. This occurred in Warsaw in January 1943, when the ghetto was surrounded and SS troops began rounding up victims for deportation. Fighting with a few smuggled or homemade weapons, residents opened fire. Fifty Germans were killed or wounded—along with many of the resistors. In the end, the SS men collected far fewer Jews for deportation than they had hoped. It was a small but significant act of resistance. In April, a much larger one would emerge in Warsaw.

"Only the Sky Has Remained Unchanged"

Many of the Jews left in the Warsaw ghetto by the spring of 1943 were members of the ZOB, the Jewish Fighters Organization. They were part of a strong underground movement of people who knew they were soon to be targeted and didn't intend to be deported without a fight.

The uprising in the Warsaw ghetto that began in April 1943 was led by 24-year-old Mordekhai Anielewicz, commander of the ZOB. His fighters were by no means trained soldiers. "The merest German private [lowest-ranking soldier]," said one, "knows more about organizing warfare than we do." Still, their motivation was great. "We have nothing more to lose," remarked one member; "we can win everything."

Although the Jews showed great courage and achieved success in the uprising, the Polish Home Army was still reluctant to supply arms to the ghetto fighters. Guns and ammunition for resistance

----

Jews captured during the Warsaw ghetto uprising are marched to a deportation site by German soldiers.

Mordekhai Anielewicz, commander of the ZOB, led the Warsaw ghetto resistance.

were in short supply, they said, and simply could not be spared. But this lack of cooperation did not stop the ZOB, the illegal government within the ghetto from preparing for an April uprising. It declared "war" on all enemies inside the ghetto, such as Gestapo agents and shop foremen who exploited Jewish workers. It kidnapped members of prominent industrial families who were profiting from the war and held them for ransom money, with which it bought guns and supplies through the underground black market.

Still, as the uprising grew nearer, Anielewicz and his small band of "desperate young men" were ill prepared to face the well-armed 6,000 German soldiers and their motorized equipment. Wrote ghetto historian Emanuel Ringelblum, "[Anielewicz] was sure that neither he nor his combatants would survive the liquidation of the Ghetto. He was sure that they would die like stray dogs and no one would even know their last resting-place." The ZOB leader was right in his prediction of death, but he was wrong about being forgotten.

Liquidation

Heinrich Himmler chose April 19, the day before Hitler's 54th birthday, as the date for the final deportation of Jews from Warsaw. Liquidation of the ghetto, Himmler reasoned, would be an ideal birthday gift for the *Führer*. The 19th was also one of the Seder nights of Passover, one of the most important religious holidays in the Jewish calendar—a night of remembrance of the Jews' Exodus from Egypt, their journey out of slavery to freedom.

It was nearly dawn when police and the SS surrounded the Warsaw ghetto. By 6:00 A.M., some 2,000 armed German soldiers had arrived with ammunition, tanks, and trucks. The ZOB fighting force, numbering about 1,000, divided into groups of 10, with no more than two women in each group. At least five were required to have their own weapons. The ZOB fired first in a fight that continued for 11 hours. When it was over, the SS retreated. The Jews still held the ghetto, and not a single one had been injured.

The ZOB fighters knew that, even though they had won the first day of the "war," the SS would be back. For the moment, however, they basked in glory. Recalled fighter Zivia Lubetkin,

> *The tomorrow did not worry us. The rejoicing amongst the Jewish fighters was great and . . . those German heroes retreated, afraid and terrorized from Jewish bombs and hand grenades, home-made.*

Tomorrow Comes

The Germans had estimated that it would take them three days to liquidate the ghetto. But at the end of day one, only about 500 Jews has been rounded up.

The second day brought more of the same. A full day of fighting resulted in not one member of the ZOB's being killed or captured. Again, only about 500 civilians were rounded up for deportation. General Jurgen Stroop, the SS man in charge, was tremendously frustrated by the resistance. In his diary, he wrote:

> *The whole* Aktion *is made more difficult by the cunning tricks employed by the Jews and bandits, e.g. it was discovered that live Jews were being taken to the Jewish cemetery in the corpse carts that collect the dead bodies lying around, and . . . escaping from the ghetto.*

The ZOB fighters were having quite another reaction. Wrote Mordekhai Anielewicz in a letter to one of his unit commanders:

> *We are aware of one thing only: what has happened has exceeded our dreams. . . . The dream of my life has become true. Jewish self defense in the Warsaw ghetto has become a fact. Jewish armed resistance and retaliation have become a reality. I have been witness to the magnificent heroic struggle of the Jewish fighters.*

Faced with this situation, General Stroop decided to burn Jews from their hideouts by setting fire to the buildings. It didn't take long for the Warsaw ghetto to become a blazing mass. Tar on the streets melted from the intense heat, "a black gooey substance overspread with sticky liquefied pieces of broken glass that stuck like glue to burning soles." But the ghetto fighters were still not defeated. Dr. Marek Edelman, a ZOB commander, later recalled:

One after another we stagger through the conflagration. From house to house, from courtyard to courtyard, with no air to breathe, with a hundred hammers clanging in our heads, with burning rafters continuously falling over us. . . .

For every new tactic the SS tried, the Jews found a way around it. The more resourceful prisoners escaped to the Aryan side of Warsaw by crawling through the city sewers. The German response to this escape route was quick. They flooded the sewers, attempting to flush out the Jews who were hiding inside the pipes. On April 27, General Stroop wrote in his diary, "It has been established by the SS men who descended the sewers that the bodies of a great many dead Jews are being washed away by the water."

When people continued to escape through the sewers, the Nazis tried smoking them out:

After some time the escapees began to scent the odor of acetone mixed with a strange sweetish smell, and simultaneously they noticed a bank of fog drifting toward them. Someone cried, "Gas!" As the civilians started to panic, their leader shouted, "Back to the bunker!". . . What they had once regarded as a hellish dungeon [the ghetto] now seemed like paradise.

One of the last groups to escape through the sewers was led by Zivia Lubetkin. Many hours later, her group emerged through the manhole outside the ghetto walls:

Captured Jews, found in a bunker during the Warsaw ghetto uprising, lie in fear as German soldiers surround them.

[We were] dirty, wrapped in rags, smeared with the filth of the sewers, faces thin and drawn, knees shaking with weakness—we were overcome with horror. Only our feverish eyes showed that we were still living human beings.

"Let Us Destroy Ourselves"

The *Aktion* that the Nazis had expected to take three days had stretched nearly into three weeks. At last, on May 8, 1943, the Germans surrounded ZOB headquarters in the ghetto. About 100 members were inside, the last remnant of this fiercely determined fighting unit. Desperate now, the fighters were spurred on by the words of Aryeh Wilner, a young resistance leader: "Come, let us destroy ourselves. Let's not fall into their hands alive."

Many followed Wilner's call for suicide. When their weapons failed, they asked their comrades to kill them. Others discovered a hidden exit through which they tried to escape, but few were successful. Still others took the route of earlier comrades— through the sewers to the Aryan side. With them were some non-fighting residents of the ghetto; in all, about 75 of them made it out alive.

A woman jumps from a burning building during the Warsaw ghetto uprising. German troops set fire to the ghetto to flush out hidden resisters.

By then, Stroop and his men were stopping at nothing to capture what they believed to be the last of 3,000 to 4,000 Jews still inside the ghetto. They began setting fire to buildings, and by May 15, only one ghetto block remained undamaged. These buildings the Nazis searched and destroyed. By evening, German forces had blown up or set fire to everything still standing, including the chapel, mortuary, and nearby buildings in the Jewish cemetery. On May 16, General Stroop wrote in his diary:

The former Jewish quarter of Warsaw is no longer in existence. With the blowing up of the Warsaw Synagogue, the Grossaktion *[major action, in this case the liquidation of the ghetto] was terminated at 20:15 hours [8:15 P.M.]. . . .*

The Aftermath

By German estimates, more than 56,000 Jews were caught or killed during the Warsaw ghetto uprising. Those captured were deported to Treblinka. The Nazis counted their casualties at 16 dead and 85 wounded. Of those Jews who escaped through the sewers or by other means, nearly 15,000 survived. Many of them managed to live through the end of the war.

". . . If there is any place [representing] more forcefully than others the tragedy of the Holocaust," wrote photo historian Ulrich Keller, "it is the Warsaw ghetto, the last refuge for hundreds of thousands of European Jews on their way to destruction by hunger, typhus and gas."

One ghetto survivor, returning to his former home in 1946, after the war, observed that "in this desert of battered bricks and twisted iron bars only the sky has remained unchanged."

CHRONOLOGY OF THE HOLOCAUST: 1933–1945

1933

January 30
Adolf Hitler becomes chancellor of Germany

February 28
Nazis declare emergency after Reichstag fire; consolidate power

March 22
Nazis open first concentration camp: Dachau

May 10
Public book burnings target works by Jews and opponents of the Nazis

July 14
Nazi Party established as one and only legal party in Germany ●●●➤

1934

January 26
German–Polish non-aggression pact signed ●●●➤

1935

September 15
Nuremberg Laws passed ●●●➤

1936

March
Germany occupies Rhineland, flouting the Versailles Treaty
⋮
↓

August
Olympic Games held in Berlin
◄●●●●

1938

November 9–10
Kristallnacht: long-planned pogrom explodes across "Greater Germany"

September 29
Munich Conference: appeasement; Allies grant Germany Sudetenland (part of Czechoslovakia)

July 6–13
Evian Conference: refugee policies

March 13
Anschluss: annexation of Austria

1937

September 7
Hitler declares end of the Versailles Treaty
◄●●●●

1939
⋮
↓

May
British White Paper: Jewish emigration to Palestine limited
●●➤

August 23
Soviet–German non-aggression pact signed

September 1
Germany invades Poland; Poland falls within a month

September 2
Great Britain and France declare war on Germany

September 17
Red (Soviet) Army invades eastern Poland

October 8
First ghetto established in Poland
⋮
↓

1941

June 22
Operation Barbarossa: invasion of the Soviet Union; German war on two fronts
⋮
↓

March 24
Germany invades North Africa

1940

October 16
Order for creation of Warsaw ghetto
◄●●●

April 27
Heinrich Himmler orders creation of Auschwitz concentration camp; established May 20

Spring
Germany conquers Denmark, Norway, Belgium, Luxembourg, Holland, and France (occupies northern part)

February 12
Deportation of Jews from Germany to occupied Poland begins

July 31
Reinhard Heydrich appointed to implement "Final Solution": extermination of European Jewry

December 7
Japan attacks Pearl Harbor

December 11
Germany and Italy declare war on the United States
●●●➤

1942

January 20
Wannsee Conference: coordination of "Final Solution"

Spring–Summer
Liquidation of Polish ghettos; deportation of Jews to extermination camps

November 19–20
Soviet Army counterattacks at Stalingrad
⋮
↓

1944

May–July
Deportation of Hungarian Jews: 437,402 sent to Auschwitz

June 6
D-Day: Allies invade Normandy

July
Soviet troops liberate Majdanek camp in Poland

October 2
Danes rescue more than 7,200 Jews from Nazis
◄●●●

June 11
Heinrich Himmler orders liquidation of all ghettos in Poland and the Soviet Union

April 19–May 16
Warsaw ghetto uprising

April 19
Bermuda Conference: fruitless discussion of rescue of Jewish victims of Nazis; liquidation of Warsaw ghetto begins

1943

January 18–21
Major act of resistance in Warsaw ghetto
◄●●●●

1945

January 27
Soviet troops liberate Auschwitz–Birkenau
●●●➤

April–May
Allies liberate Buchenwald, Bergen-Belsen, Dachau, Mauthausen, and Theresienstadt concentration camps

April 30
Hitler commits suicide

May 7
Germany surrenders unconditionally to Allies

May 8
V-E Day: Victory in Europe
⋮
↓

November
Nuremberg Trials begin

Glossary

Aktion The German word for an "action" or plan of action. When used by the SS or Gestapo, it often meant the roundup or murder of Jews.

Anti-Semite A person who hates Jews.

Antisemitism Hatred of Jews.

Concentration Camps Labor camps set up by the Nazis to house political prisoners or people they considered to be "undesirable." Prisoners were made to work like slaves and many died as a result of starvation, disease, or beatings. *Also called work camps, work centers, and prison camps.*

Crematorium A building in the camps that contained the ovens, where the bodies of victims were burned. The term is sometimes used to refer to the ovens themselves.

Deportation Shipment of victims to death or concentration camps, usually by train in unheated or cooled cattle cars.

Einsatzgruppen "Special Action Groups"— mobile killing squads that followed the German Army through Eastern Europe for the purpose of killing Jews.

Einsatzkommando Commando units that carried out killing operations, particularly of groups of Jews who were to be exterminated in gas vans or by firing squads.

Extermination Camps Death camps built by the Nazis in German-occupied Poland for the sole purpose of killing "enemies" of the Third Reich. The victims' bodies were usually burned in ovens (crematoria). The six extermination camps were Auschwitz–Birkenau, Belzec, Chelmno, Majdanek, Sobibór, and Treblinka. *Also called killing centers.*

Final Solution The Nazis' plan to destroy all European Jews.

Genocide The deliberate killing of a racial, cultural, or political group.

Gentile A non-Jewish person.

Gestapo The Nazi secret police, who were responsible for rounding up, arresting, and deporting victims to ghettos or camps. The Gestapo were part of the SS.

Ghetto In Hitler's Europe, the section of a city where Jews were forced to live apart from other groups, in conditions of extreme crowding and deprivation.

Holocaust A term for the state-sponsored, systematic persecution and annihilation of European Jewry by Nazi Germany and its collaborators between 1933 and 1945. While Jews were the primary victims, with approximately 6 million murdered, many other groups were targeted, including Romani, the mentally and physically disabled, Soviet prisoners of war, political dissidents, Jehovah's Witnesses, and male homosexuals. It is believed that perhaps 4 million non-Jews were killed under the Nazi regime.

Jews People who belong to the religion of Judaism.

Judenrat "Jewish Council," a group of Jews selected by the Germans to run the ghettos. Often these Jews were promised favors for themselves and their families for serving.

Judenrein "Purified of Jews," a German expression for Hitler's plan to rid Germany of all Jews.

Liberation The act of freeing the Nazis' victims from death and concentration camps at the end of the war.

Liquidation The removal of residents from the ghettos, concentration camps or extermination camps.

Nazi A member of the Nazi Party or something associated with the party, such as "Nazi government."

Palestine A region in the Middle East, part of which is now known as Israel. Palestine was controlled by the British government from 1922 to 1948.

Partisans Bands of independent fighters who lived in the woods or other remote areas and harassed the German army or the SS in an effort to disrupt their actions.

Resettlement The term the Nazis used to make Jews think they were being transported to work camps in Eastern Europe, when in actuality they were being taken to extermination camps.

Resistance Action taken against the Nazis by Jews or other victims of SS terror. Members of resistance groups worked "underground" in secrecy.

Selection The process of choosing which victims at the death camps would be spared to work and which ones would be killed immediately.

SA From the German term *Sturmabteilungen,* meaning "stormtroopers." The SA were Nazi soldiers. *Also called brown-shirts.*

SS From the German term *Schutzstaffel,* meaning "defense unit." The SS began as Hitler's personal bodyguard and developed into the most powerful and feared organization in the Third Reich. *Also called black-shirts.*

Third Reich *Reich* means "empire." In German history, the first Reich lasted from 962 until 1806, the second from 1871 to 1918. In the early 1920s, Hitler began using the term "Third Reich" to describe his own regime, which lasted from 1933 to 1945.

Untermenschen A German word meaning "sub-humans" or lesser human beings. Used by the Nazis to refer to Jews, Gypsies, Jehovah's Witnesses, homosexuals, the physically and mentally ill, and the Nazis' political enemies.

Volkisch A "people's movement" based on a fear and hatred of foreigners, particularly Jews, and that believed in the superiority of the Germanic race.

ZOB An acronym formed from the Polish name *Zydowska Organizacja Bojowa*: "Jewish Fighters Organization." The ZOB organized resistance in the Warsaw ghetto.

Source Notes

Introduction:
Page 10: "...cold-hearted, shameless...." Adolf Hitler. *Mein Kampf*. Boston: Houghton Mifflin, 1971, p.59.

Page 10: "The Jew must clear out of Europe...." Eleanor H. Ayer. *The Importance of Adolf Hitler*. San Diego: Lucent Books, Inc., 1996, p. 84.

Page 11: "The Popes of the Third Reich...." Gerald Simons, ed. *The Nazis*. Chicago: Time-Life Books, 1980, p. 143.

Chapter 1:
Page 16: "I couldn't speak...." Konnilyn Feig. *Hitler's Death Camps*. New York: Holmes & Meier, 1979, p. 271.

Page 18: "The people...." Azriel Eisenberg. *Witness to the Holocaust*. New York: Pilgrim Press, 1981, p. 269.

Page 18: "The furnace could hold...." Feig, pp. 271–272.

Page 18: "...the proper attitude...." Robert Payne. *The Life and Death of Adolf Hitler*. New York: Praeger Publishers, 1973, p. 131.

Page 19: "...advisable to eliminate the Jews...." Leni Yahil. *The Holocaust*. New York: Oxford University Press, 1990, pp. 312, 315.

Page 19: "For the moment...." Martin Gilbert. *The Holocaust*. New York: Holt, Rinehart & Winston, 1985, p. 282.

Page 19: "...the Crimea is purged...." Martin Gilbert. *Atlas of the Holocaust*. Oxford, England: Pergamon Press, 1988, p. 86.

Page 20: "Persons to be executed...." William L. Shirer. *The Rise and Fall of the Third Reich*. New York: Simon & Schuster, 1960, p. 960.

Page 22: "Why do you worry so much...." Nechama Tec. *Defiance: The Bielski Partisans*. New York: Oxford University Press, 1993, pp. 45, 46.

Chapter 2:
Page 25: "...Old people's transport...." Eisenberg, p. 318.

Page 26: "Old German Jews...." Feig, p. 245.

Page 26: "Many times a day...." Feig, p. 247.

Page 27: "The common report...." Feig, p. 277.

Page 30: "...they herded us...." Claude Lanzmann. *Shoah*. New York: Pantheon Books, 1985, pp. 57–59.

Page 30–31: "May 6...." Simon Wiesenthal. *Every Day Remembrance Day*. New York: Henry Holt & Company, 1986, pp. 108–110.

Page 31: "Men and women were separated...." Helen Waterford. *Commitment to the Dead*. Frederick, CO: Renaissance House Publishers, 1987, p. 57.

Page 32: "I witnessed scenes...." Ilya Ehrenburg & Vasily Grossman. *The Black Book*. New York: Holocaust Library, 1981, pp. 438–439.

Page 32: "...men, fourteen to sixty...." Gilbert, *Atlas*, p. 99.

Page 33: "...In any event...." Gilbert, *The Holocaust*, p. 363.

Page 33: "...a dramatic symbol...." Callum Mac-Donald. *The Killing of SS Obergruppenführer Reinhard Heydrich*. New York: The Free Press, 1989, p. 184.

Chapter 3:
Page 35: "I hear a lot of noise...." Yitzchak Mais, ed. *A Day in the Warsaw Ghetto*. Jerusalem: Yad Vashem, 1988, unnumbered p. 1.

Page 36: "It is a desolate building." Ulrich Keller, ed. *The Warsaw Ghetto in Photos*. New York: Dover Publications, 1984, p. xii.

Page 37: "The most fearful sight...." Lucy S. Dawidowicz. *The War Against the Jews*. New York: Bantam Books, 1975, p. 281.

Page 37: "Of all the gruesome scenes...." Eisenberg, p. 306.

Page 37: "There would be five or six...." Keller, p. xv.

Page 38: "There are a great number...." Mais, unnumbered p. 19.

Page 39: "When I asked...." Gilbert, *The Holocaust*, p. 389.

Page 39: "The SS wants me...." Michael Berenbaum. *The World Must Know*. Boston: Little, Brown, 1993, p. 79.

Page 39: "I am powerless...." Dawidowicz, p. 408.

Page 39: "...Too late...." Berenbaum, p. 79.

Page 41: "The orphans were clutching...." Berenbaum, pp. 79–80.

Page 41: "This was no march...." Berenbaum, p. 80.

Chapter 4:

Page 43: "She takes my arm...." Eisenberg, p. 229.

Page 43: "In Auschwitz...." David A. Adler. *We Remember the Holocaust*. New York: Henry Holt, 1989, pp. 76–77.

Page 44: "Suddenly someone pushed Olek...." Mania Halevi. "Give Me Shelter for the Night." Unpublished manuscript, pp. 22–23.

Page 47: "Jews...don't walk...." Gilbert, *The Holocaust*, p. 127.

Page 47–48: "...in the interest of the security...." Gilbert, *The Holocaust*, p. 387.

Page 49: "I have never been able...." David Kahane. *Lvov Ghetto Diary*. Amherst, MA: University of Massachusetts Press, 1990, p. 62.

Page 49: "When it came time to separate them...." Gilbert, *The Holocaust*, p. 459.

Chapter 5:

Page 52: "I've never been able...." Claudine Vegh. *I Didn't Say Goodbye*. New York: E.P. Dutton, 1979, p.133.

Page 52: "Nobody knows...." Wiesenthal, p. 214.

Page 53: "As we have no...." Robert Goralski. *World War II Almanac 1931–1945*. New York: Bonanza Books, 1981, p. 69.

Page 53: "...to exterminate all Jews...." Berenbaum, p. 161.

Page 53: "What we did...." Berenbaum, p. 163.

Pages 54–55: "Deportees arrived at Auschwitz...." Berenbaum, p. 119.

Page 54: "When the prisoners arrived...." Feig, pp. 119–120.

Page 55: "...eyes were opened...." Ayer, p. 26.

Page 55: "...that the inmates...." Gordon J. Horwitz. *In the Shadow of Death*. New York: The Free Press, 1990, p. 51.

Page 56: "During stone-breaking...." Horwitz, p. 38.

Page 56: "The chemical used...." Adler, p. 77.

Page 57: "It is the silence...." Anne Frank. *The Diary of a Young Girl*. Garden City, NY: Doubleday, 1967, p. 32.

Page 57: "The next two nights...." Waterford, p. 43.

Page 57: "After a short visit...." Waterford, pp. 43–44.

Chapter 6:

Page 60: "Every nation...." Richard Lukas. *The Forgotten Holocaust*. Lexington: University of Kentucky Press, 1986, p. 34.

Page 60: "A new wave of terror...." Lukas, pp. 34–35.

Page 60: "We have thousands...." Lukas, p. 37.

Page 61: "...they did not like us Jews...." Alan Levy. *The Wiesenthal File*. Grand Rapids, MI: William B. Eerdmans Publishing, 1993, pp. 26–27.

Page 61: "[Poles] who saved Jews...." Gilbert, *The Holocaust*, pp. 660–661.

Page 62: "When we disembarked...." U.S. Holocaust Memorial Museum Identification Card #1221.

Page 63: "Living under the constant threat...." Jan Yoors. *Crossing*. New York: Simon & Schuster, 1971, p. 138.

Page 63: "...shot or starved...." Gilbert, *The Holocaust*, p. 824.

Page 64: "...guilty, guilty, guilty!" Barbara Rogasky. *Smoke and Ashes*. New York: Holiday House, 1988, pp. 150–151.

Page 64: " ...a false doctrine...." Feig, p. 25.

Chapter 7:

Page 67: "The merest German private...." Rogasky, p. 114.

Page 68: "[Anielewicz] was sure...." Joseph Kermish, ed. *To Live with Honor and Die with Honor*. Jerusalem: Yad Vashem, 1986, p. 600.

Page 69: "The tomorrow did not...." Berenbaum, p. 110.

Page 69: "The whole *Aktion*...." Eisenberg, p. 405.

Page 69: "We are aware...." Berenbaum, p. 110.

Page 70: "...a black gooey substance...." Dan Kurzman. *The Bravest Battle*. New York: G.P. Putnam's Sons, 1976, p. 162.

Page 70: "One after another...." Kurzman, p. 162.

Page 70: "It has been established...." Eisenberg, p. 406.

Page 70: "After some time...." Kurzman, p. 262.

Page 71: "[We were] dirty...." Eisenberg, p. 404.

Page 71: "Come, let us...." Berenbaum, p. 112.

Page 72: "The former Jewish quarter..." Eisenberg, p. 408.

Page 72: "If there is any place...." Ulrich, p. vii.

Page 72: "...in this desert...." Ulrich, p. vii.

Further Reading

David Adler. *We Remember the Holocaust*. New York: Henry Holt and Company, 1989.

Eleanor H. Ayer. *The Importance of Adolf Hitler*. San Diego: Lucent Books, 1996.

Eleanor H. Ayer. *Parallel Journeys*. New York: Atheneum, 1995.

Eleanor H. Ayer. *The United States Holocaust Memorial Museum: America Keeps the Memory Alive*. New York: Macmillan, 1994.

Michael Berenbaum. *The World Must Know*. Boston: Little, Brown, 1993.

Anne Frank. *Diary of a Young Girl*. Garden City, NY: Doubleday, 1967.

Martin Gilbert. *Atlas of the Holocaust*. Oxford, England: Pergamon Press, 1988.

Ulrich Keller, ed. *The Warsaw Ghetto in Photographs*. New York: Dover Publications, 1984.

Lambert and Bow. *The Holocaust* [A compact disc]. Minneapolis: Quanta Press, 1994.

Claude Lanzmann. *Shoah: An Oral History of the Holocaust*. New York: Pantheon Books, 1985.

Yitzchak Mais. *A Day in the Warsaw ghetto*. Jerusalem: Yad Vashem, 1988.

Barbara Rogasky. *Smoke and Ashes*. New York: Holiday House, 1988.

Claudine Vegh. *I Didn't Say Goodbye*. New York: E.P. Dutton, 1984.

Hana Volavkova & the United States Holocaust Memorial Council. *I Never Saw Another Butterfly*. New York: Schocken Books, 1993.

Elie Wiesel. *Night*. New York: Bantam Books, 1960.

Simon Wiesenthal. *Every Day Remembrance Day*. New York: Henry Holt and Company, 1986.

Bibliography

Eleanor H. Ayer. *The Importance of Adolf Hitler*. San Diego: Lucent Books, Inc., 1996.

Michael Berenbaum. *The World Must Know*. Boston: Little, Brown, 1993.

Lucy S. Dawidowicz. *The War Against the Jews*. New York: Bantam, 1975.

Ilya Ehrenburg & Vasily Grossman, eds. *The Black Book*. New York: Holocaust Library, 1980.

Azriel Eisenberg. *Witness to the Holocaust*. New York: The Pilgrim Press, 1981.

Konnilyn Feig. *Hitler's Death Camps*. New York: Holmes & Meier, 1979.

Martin Gilbert. *The Atlas of the Holocaust*. Oxford, England: Pergamon Press, 1988.

Martin Gilbert. *The Holocaust*. New York: Holt, Rinehart & Winston, 1985.

Anton Gill. *The Journey Back From Hell*. New York: William Morrow, 1988.

Robert Goralski. *World War II Almanac 1931–1945*. New York: Bonanza Books, 1981.

Mania Halevi. "Give Me Shelter For the Night." Unpublished manuscript.

Adolf Hitler. *Mein Kampf*. Boston: Houghton Mifflin, 1971.

Gordon J. Horwitz. *In the Shadow of Death*. New York: The Free Press, 1990.

Identification Card #1221. Washington, D.C.: United States Holocaust Memorial Museum.

David Kahane. *Lvov Ghetto Diary*. Amherst, MA: University of Massachusetts Press, 1990.

Ulrich Keller, ed. *The Warsaw Ghetto in Photos*. New York: Dover Publications, 1984.

Joseph Kermish, ed. *To Live With Honor and Die With Honor*. Jerusalem: Yad Vashem, 1986.

Hanna Krall. *Shielding the Flame*. New York: Henry Holt and Company, 1986.

Dan Kurzman. *The Bravest Battle*. New York: G.P. Putnam's Sons, 1976.

Claude Lanzmann. *Shoah*. New York: Pantheon Books, 1985.

Alan Levy. *The Wiesenthal File*. Grand Rapids, MI: William B. Eerdmans Publishing, 1993.

Richard C. Lukas. *The Forgotten Holocaust*. Lexington, KY: University Press of Kentucky, 1986.

Callum MacDonald. *The Killing of SS Obergruppenführer Reinhard Heydrich*. New York: Macmillan, 1989.

Yitzchak Mais. *A Day in the Warsaw Ghetto*. Jerusalem: Yad Vashem, 1988.

Zdenka Novak. *When Heaven's Vault Cracked*. Devon, England: Merlin Books, 1995.

Robert Payne. *The Life and Death of Adolf Hitler*. New York: Praeger, 1973.

Barbara Rogasky. *Smoke and Ashes*. New York: Holiday House, 1988.

William L. Shirer. *The Rise and Fall of the Third Reich*. New York: Simon & Schuster, 1960.

Gerald Simons, ed. *The Nazis*. Chicago: Time-Life Books, 1980.

Nechama Tec. *Defiance: The Bielski Partisans*. New York: Oxford University Press, 1993.

Claudine Vegh. *I Didn't Say Goodbye*. New York: E.P. Dutton, 1979.

Helen Waterford. *Commitment to the Dead*. Frederick, CO: Renaissance House Publishers, 1987.

Simon Wiesenthal. *Every Day Remembrance Day*. New York: Henry Holt & Company, 1986.

Leni Yahil. *The Holocaust: The Fate of European Jewry*. New York: Oxford University Press, 1990.

Jan Yoors. *Crossing*. New York: Simon & Schuster, 1971.

Index

Photo Credits

Cover and pages 49, 50, 51, 66, 67, 71: National Archives, courtesy of USHMM Photo Archives; pages 8, 9, 20 (bottom), 46: YIVO Institute for Jewish Research, courtesy of USHMM Photo Archives; page 11: KZ Gedenkstatte Dachau, courtesy of USHMM Photo Archives; pages 12, 13: Henryk Ross, YIVO Institute for Jewish Research, courtesy of USHMM Photo Archives; pages 15 (top), 22, 41, 68: Yad Vashem Photo Archives, courtesy of USHMM Photo Archives; page 15 (bottom): Jewish Historical Institute, courtesy of USHMM Photo Archives; page 17: Novosty Press, courtesy of USHMM Photo Archives; page 20 (top left): Harry Lore, courtesy of USHMM Photo Archives; page 20 (top right): Main Commission for the Investigation of Nazi War Crimes, courtesy of USHMM Photo Archives; pages 24, 25: Joint Distribution Committee; page 26: Sharon Muller, courtesy of USHMM Photo Archives; page 31: Rijkinstituut vor Oologsdocumentatie, courtesy of USHMM Photo Archives; pages 34, 35: State Archives of the Russian Federation, courtesy of USHMM Photo Archives; page 36: Archiwum Akt Nowych [Former Communist Party Archives], courtesy of USHMM Photo Archives; page 37: Prof. Leopold Pfefferberg-Page, courtesy of USHMM Photo Archives; page 39: Ghetto Fighters' House, courtesy of USHMM Photo Archives; pages 42, 43: Gedenkstate Buchenwald, courtesy of USHMM Photo Archives; page 57 (upper): ©AFF/AFS Amsterdam the Netherlands; page 57 (lower): AP/Wide World Photos; pages 58, 59: Bildarchiv Preussischer Kulturbesitz, courtesy of USHMM Photo Archives; page 62: Arnold Kramer, courtesy of USHMM Photo Archives; page 65: Dr. George Wittenstein, courtesy of USHMM Photo Archives; page 72: Louis Gonda, courtesy of USHMM Photo Archives.

All maps and graphs ©Blackbirch Press, Inc.